The Clear Shadow

The Clear Shadow
Mary Casey

RIGBY & LEWIS

First published by Rigby & Lewis Easter morning 1992

Rigby & Lewis Publishing (Capedawn Ltd.)
20, Springfield Road, Southgate, Crawley,
West Sussex, RH11 8AD, England

Copyright © Gerard Casey 1992

Foreword © Charles Lock 1991

'Arul' Copyright © Anna Dimascio

Study for a portrait of Mary Casey in 1972 by Judith Shackleton ©

ISBN 1 869887 12 3

ALL RIGHTS RESERVED

Printed in Great Britain by Redwood Press Limited, Melksham, Wiltshire

The Publishers are profoundly thankful to Louise de Bruin

The Publishers wish to express especial regards and gratitude also to:
Richard Wilson, the late G. Wilson Knight, Frank Kibblewhite, Griffin Beale, Leonard H. Rickett, Michael Kidston, Christopher Arnold, Arya Parker, Barry Barstow, Doug and Margo Kite

Acknowledgements are due to *The Enitharmon Press* which first published 'Full Circle' and 'Christophoros'.
'Full Circle' and 'Christophoros' are here revised.

Mary Casey was born in Hampshire in 1915 and passed her childhood and youth in that county at Horsebridge Mill near Romsey which was owned and run by her father Hounsell Penny. Her mother Lucy Amelia was the youngest daughter of the Rev. C. F. Powys, Vicar of Montacute in Somerset. She shared the love of nature and literature of his distinguished family.

In 1945 she married and soon after was found to be suffering from tuberculosis. The disease remained a health problem throughout her life but was brought under control after she went with her husband in 1946 to live on her uncle's farm in Kenya. This book of poems is dedicated to her uncle and godfather William Powys, with whom she had a very close relationship rooted in a deep mutual understanding. In 1976 she returned to England and lived in Dorset until her death in 1980.

She also wrote three historical novels, one of which, *The Kingfisher's Wing* based on the life of Plotinus, was published in 1987 by Rigby & Lewis.

For W.E.P.

the old man's house stands at the edge of the gorge
where boulders with broken fangs buttress the steep
in the bottom the river runs loud with rocks
in a cavernous gloom of glowering trees
there is the grove of bananas a temple
with smooth columns gold and black that hold aloft
fluted vaulted roof of ribbed green leaves bearing
clumsy loads of fruit clusters here on bare
dug ground the old man comes to walk with the sound
of waterfall mill-wheel and liquid singing
of birds and beyond and beyond the river
the waterless land and the western rampart
of hills eastward white plains reach to meet the sun
rising over the rim of an empty land
northward the desert the washing hangs on blue
mountains blue isles in a far cloud-shadowed sea

the room where he sleeps looks west to the evening
hills here the bed of his father and mother
here the pictures of wife dead and son dead and
the bundles of letters of brothers dead and
sisters dead that he takes from the deep chest
deep to hold all the filled full years of his life

south the mountain south the sky-bearing pillar
nurse of keen snow unchanging from age to age
heart of the land heart of his life which his hand
has given us in all its sky-born moods
a thousand times with cattle with sheep
with forest dead tree gazelle   his homage this
to life-giving earth he has wielded for God

(As I wrote this the emerald-spotted wood-dove was calling. Africans think the bird says, 'father dead, mother dead, wife dead, brothers dead, sisters dead ... children dead ... all dead ... dead ... dead ... dead ...')

Contents

Foreword by *Charles Lock* — 15

Meditation for Avicenna — 25

Full Circle — 27

Dawn	29	The Slate Pencil	50
Full Circle	29	'Herz Mein Herz'	51
The Aeolian Bell	30	In This Alone	52
Windy Hill	30	Helios and Hades	52
Nests	31	The Scarlet Swan	53
The Pool	32	Remembrance	54
Cuckoo	32	To – in Africa	55
The Snipe	33	To a Silver Locket	55
Cuckoo-clock	33	'Are those your Tears'	55
Northwardbound	34	Vintage	56
A Nightbird's Cry	35	Lost	56
After Reading Basho	35	'When you look at me...'	57
'As a Sparrow'	35	O Give to my Bones	58
Caprice	35	Sunt Lacrimae Rerum	58
Heart Burial	36	Pierian	59
Eden	36	Restoration	59
Out of the Ground	36	After a Reading of *East Coker*	60
Frost	37	Not after Plutarch	61
Hogmanay Eve	37	From Whom no Secrets are Hid	62
Water-wheel	38	When after the Cold	63
Dennis Davis	39	The Rustle	63
Centenary	40	'He brought me to the House of Wine'	64
Dionysus	41	Maud	65
Fresco	41	At the Window	66
After the Storm	42	Odyssey	67
Edith in Africa	43	Phlegethon	67
Mockery Gap	44	A Journey into Wales	68
The Rains Begin	44	Tao	70
For Peter	45	Composure	71
Upanishad	46	On Missing Plotinus	72
Who are Aware...	47	'Just at Dawn'	73
To Alyse's Brooch	48	Sirakoi	74
Topaz	48	Urchin	75
For Charles	49		
For D.F.C.	50		

Christophoros

Part One	78
Christophoros	79
Meditation	
on Reading the Old Testament	80
My Son	80
Nothing is without a Part in Soul	81
Moses	82
Wilderness	84
The Baptist	90
Annunciation	94
Birth	97
Epiphany	98
Meditation of St. Joseph	102
Snowstorm	103
Transfiguration	104
'For the Water of the	
Well of Bethlehem'	106
Maundy	107
Good Friday	108
Mary	110
Atonement	111
Four Meditations for Easter	112
Easter Day	116
Part Two	120
Crucifixion	121
The Mantis	122
'Ah, my Dear, be Satisfied'	122
'Even the loudly Roaring Lions'	123
In Darkness	123
Epigrams	124
The Word	124
Calvary	125
'As having Nothing...'	125
'Sand Grains and Grasses	
Prophesy'	126
One White Flower	126
Nenuphar	127
At the Ngare Ndare	127
'It is Hard for Thee...'	128
Adrad	129
Road to Emmaus	130
Redemption	130
Atonement	131
'Behold, the Heaven...'	132
Christening	133
Easter	134
Easter Sunday	134
The Quick and the Dead	135
Village Church	136
Burning Bush	137
'There lithe a Knight...'	137
The Trinity of Rublev	138
The Choir	139
A Meditation on Angels	140
'And Never and Never to Die'	140
Phoenix	141
Logos	142
The Chariot	143
ἑαυτῷ δὲ λαλείτω καὶ τῷ Θεῷ	144
The Mind of Christ	145

Geometrical Relationships 147

Africa	148
The Beale	149
Springs Cottage	150
Thesiger at Springs Cottage	151
Fig Tree	152
Sally's Dream	153
The Broken Flute	154
Epigram	154
For Marian	155
Conies	155
A Pair of Bushbuck	156
The Leveret on Lizard Hill	157
Friend Hare	157
Now I am Quiet	158
The Unvisited Noose	158
Scheltopusik	159
Chrysococcyx	159
Mountain Wagtail	160
Green-backed Heron	160
Speke's Weaver's Chantry	161
L'Après-midi	162
Turtur Chalkosphilos	162
Narina's Trogon	163
Open Sky	163
Tristram	164
Acacia Thorn	164
The Whistling Thorn	165
Rounding Musunguka	165
Cosmic Gnosis	166
Thirst	166
Abyssinian Long-claw	167
Kenya	167
Sunday afternoon	168
Bogo and Springy	168
Fulfilled	169
The Life-giving Earth	170
Hogmanay Eve	171
Modulations	172
For K.P.	173
T.F.P.	174
Offerings	174
No More	175
For May at Montacute	176
Katey Grey	176
Sibylline	176
Dryad	177
Bramleys	177
Wizard	178
Warrior	179
Still Pauses	180
Wanderers	180
Winds of Spring	181
Wind-hover	181
Jessed	182
An Instant Single	182
Hedgehog	183
The Visit	183
The Falling Star	184
Calyx	184
Festival	185
The Saint	185
The Twins	186
Nectary	186
No Stones	187
Meditation on the Eve of Christ's Nativity	188
The Unseen Bird	189
Chinese	189
The Nature	190
Flown	190
Unbrailable	191
Wisp of Snipe	191
For a Bird Dying on a Love-letter	192
Greek	193
Paean	193
The Vesture of Fog	194
μκρά χαῖρε	195
Kouros	196
Epigrams for a Young Girl Dead	197
'Behind the Mill'	198
Free	198
No Threads Cut	199
Chinese Poems	199
Jack-go-to-bed-at-noon	201
The Undivined Response	201
For R.S. Thomas	202
Auden Dead	202
Over the River	203
Nebelglanz	203
Geometrical Relationships	204
Pain	204
Fog	205

Foreword

There are poets for whom communication with others is not of the same urgency as expression. For some poets publication, and the response of readers, is as integral as composition to the process and nature of being a poet; other poets resist publication, sensing therein an exploitation and a betrayal. Of those poets who were entirely successful in their resistance, who were known as poets only posthumously, Traherne and Hopkins are among the most eminent. It is no coincidence that both these poets were priests, and that their poetry was entirely subordinate to their vocation, an act of private devotion, of communication with God rather than with readers, a privilege of response not lightly to be divulged.

During her life-time Mary Casey had been persuaded to publish only a handful of her poems, always in journals of limited circulation. On her death, in January 1980, she left behind a large body of work, from which three sequences of poetry have been selected. The first, 'Full Circle', consists largely of poems which are personal in both occasion and theme, meditations about friends, dedicated to friends. 'Christophoros' unfolds as a religious sequence that explicates the faith which informs Mary Casey's vision. 'Geometrical Relationships' more directly addresses the empirical, the tough daily routine of the poet's life, and in these poems we must listen to the quiet notes of suggestion and implication.

Mary Casey's poetry has many modes, and it is one of the great satisfactions of a poet who may be thought to be essentially mystical in vision and language, that she is as adept at saying as at not saying. Sometimes her poetry can be symbolic, her idiom scripturally allusive, as in 'Dennis Davis'. This poem from 'Full Circle' celebrates a character recalled from Mary Casey's rural childhood in Hampshire, and it transforms a knacker into an exemplar of Christ's teaching. Such a poem risks the reduction of a person to a mere cipher, but the poet avoids this by taking her figurative cue from the knacker himself:

> bread's all right he said
> but you want something with it

This is gently modulated into the last line, when the poet's father shares some wine with the knacker:

> he brought Dennis in poured him glass
> after glass and he drank to the years
> of bread alone

Here the colloquial is fused perfectly with the resonantly symbolic.

Mary Casey releases words, allows them to convey more than their quotidian sense; so, looking, she sees more than appears, has access to the symbolic. As a 'visionary' she understands well the betrayal of that word's etymology, and of the etymology of its synonym 'seer'; explicitly in 'After a Reading of *East Coker*':

> for the poet who is seer
> (things invisible to see)

What is presented to the poet's eye, 'receiving simply the image', is inadequate until it has been assumed into a vision. Much of Mary Casey's adult life was spent in Kenya, and many of these poems were written there; its particular atmospheric qualities are both source and complement of her power of looking:

> I hold my hands a wimple for my eyes
> that I may see the vision of the day
> the egrets in the trees the six
> white swan-white triangles in-
> verted sails
> the heaven washed new
> and earth a paradise
> diamonded in clear shining after rain
> ('After the Storm')

Through that clear shining the poet throws on all things the illumination of the symbolic.

It is most obvious in the poems of 'Christophoros', but evident in all her work, that Mary Casey looked habitually on the world with a sacramental attention. For her, a symbol does not stand for something else; for all that it illuminates of the transcendental, a symbol remains integrated in the natural, real world. Her poetry unfolds the immaterial implications of the material, that which would remain covert to those who, having eyes, see not; those who look, but are not seers.

One of 'Full Circle''s most finely-wrought poems, 'Frost', loads that thin brief covering of nature with a weight of symbols that it well sustains:

> frost with scriptural cold
> writes all the moonlight night

The etymological play that connects 'scriptural' with 'writes' serves to endorse the poem's visual layering, while at the same time heightening the tentativeness of the poem's construction. That the last four lines are not quite welded syntactically gives point to the frailty of frost and all that is signifies:

> when across the turquoise sky
> spreads the red of sun
> cold of chiselled history
> frost is all undone

The word 'history' is used here with chiselled precision, for it uncovers yet another element in the complex of 'writing' and 'scripture', all, as it were, bound up by that which will be their undoing. Richly intricate significance is seen, 'visioned', in frost, and conveyed through the apparent simplicity of a chiefly monosyllabic vocabulary and a rhythm precariously close to doggerel. It is a most daring poem and a great accomplishment.

'Christophoros' is a sequence of religious poems, an imagination and a bearing of Christianity: 'our God-bearing fathers' are not only the saints but every forger of a link in the tradition. The personification of St. Christopher, as a particularised, historical individual, is an attenuation of this concept which Mary Casey, by her title, seeks to avoid. Her sacramental vision goes further: despite the primacy of the believer, of the participator in worship and prayer, Christ-bearing is not restricted to the human. Things, objects in the created world, are possessed of a symbolic continuity which, throughout history, links human vision to the divine: indeed, it might be said that this is how history is constituted. This understanding of vision and faith, which is to be found throughout Mary Casey's poetry, entrusts much to the imagination.

Of all Christ-bearing energies in creation Mary Casey celebrates light as the 'first and best symbol'. Not only is Christ the light of the world, but only by light can we see the world. We ourselves, in a haunting line from the first poem of the sequence, are 'castaways on the coasts of light'. In almost all these poems light is explicitly present, as if it could not be avoided, and yet must never be taken for granted. Three orders of light appear to be distinguished, of which the lowest is the 'clear light of the mind', bequeathed to us by the Greeks, which, when taken as all-sufficient, is associated with Lucifer ('Four Meditations for Easter II', 'One White Flower'). The highest order is the absolute light of the divine: 'in heaven light runs through light' ('Epiphany II'). In Orthodox theology the visibility of icons symbolises the uncreated light, light which requires no body or surface or reflection for its manifestation. Rublev's icon of the Trinity is here described in terms of the negation of other forms of light, the ordinary light of day which depends on shadow. Uncreated light, as the extreme opposite of darkness, must negate that light in whose shadings the darkness is implicated; and language stumbles:

> on them falls not the light
> as earth turns towards day
> the light that falls as weight
> on our opaque clay
>
> ('The Trinity of Rublev')

Uncreated light takes no verb.

The light of reason and the light of heaven both lead the poet towards abstraction, where the appropriate discourse would be philosophical or theological. The poetic imagination looks to the 'middle order' of light, the light of creation, the light bound up with shadows and turnings; where a vision is that which is seen, and a seer is one who uses his eyes. In these meditations on the light of creation the arch-instance is the Transfiguration. A poem on this subject opens with Newton's question:

> among such various and strange transmutations
> why may not Nature change bodies into light
> and light into bodies?
>
> ('Transfiguration II')

Transfigured, Christ's clay is not opaque, for the disciples saw both light and body, spirit and matter, divine and human, at once. Yet it is a property of light, an aspect of Nature, not a creation-scorning miracle, that light can be both origin and reflection. According to St. Gregory Palamas, 'God is called Light, not with reference to His essence, but to His energy'; in Mary Casey's

'Transfiguration' the light in Christ, the light that is Christ, seems to bind and encompass both essence and energy. The same poem cites A.N. Whitehead: 'the quanta of energy pass into vibrations of light.' Discreetly, the poetic and the spiritual are shown to be latent in the language of science: the idea is entertained that the wave/particle conundrum of quantum physics is an analogue of the Incarnation and the Transfiguration, of the mystery of Christ at once fully human and fully divine.

Poetry itself can be an analogue of the Christian mysteries. Looking back to David and Solomon, archetypal poets of the Judaeo-Christian tradition, we find 'poetry kindled in the deepest dark', in a poem tellingly named 'Meditation on reading the Old Testament'. But poetry and light should not be too easily or glibly equated, for this must always be remembered: 'we know light has no tongue' ('Epiphany III'). Thus in a brilliant epigram Mary Casey sums up the ancient conundrum of the visionary and his language. The privilege of divine intimation conflicts with the human need to express and communicate, the temptation to utterance. Poets less reticent, more defiant than St. Paul, who 'heard unspeakable words, which it is not lawful for man to utter', strive in all tact and faithfulness to reconcile the vision and the word, to lend voice to light. Each achievement of the poet is a new incarnation and a new transfiguration:

> intensity of being
> the passion of poetry
> the light that shone in the word
> ('In Darkness')

A faith which derives such inspiration from light is intensely sacramental, for the light which came into the world receives no more attention than the creation made visible by that light – made after the light, yet whose opaque surfaces alone render light visible. As long as the symbol and the fact of light, in all its complexities whether physical or metaphysical, is held in remembrance and in sight, the mysteries of incarnation and transfiguration are perpetuated, renewed.

Mary Casey is not a poet of theological abstraction, for in her sacramental vision light and bodies are interchangeable; and most vitally for a poet, the words for bodies remain valid for transfigured bodies, the light shining in the word as in the body. The language of spirit is, transfigured, lit, the language of matter. Only by describing things, by attending rigorously to matter, can the poet re-kindle the guttering light of image and symbol in the decadence of abstraction.

Some of the most memorable poems in the 'Christophoros' sequence take Biblical subjects and, by a reflexive extension of vision, augment the familiar accounts. It is notably the quiet characters of the Bible who leave scope for the poets who come after. St. Joseph, always peripheral to narratives and paintings of the Nativity, meditates colloquially, as if from within a painting: 'I am glad I bought that blue robe for our bridal', thus authorising, by historical explanation, the colour in which the Virgin has customarily been depicted in western European art, since at least the tenth century. At the same time we are reminded that the symbolism of the Virgin's blue robe may be an accretion on a fact as banal as a matter of Joseph's taste.

It is one thing to give voice to those who are silent; but it takes enormous tact and involves many risks, to invent another speech for Moses:

> Lord God give this last vision to my eyes
> cracked to the quick by fire and furnace suns
> to feel from the grave's edge Thy heritage
> ('Moses I')

These words somehow achieve the appropriate weight and authority, and that last line magnificently sustains its speaker.

Essential to Mary Casey's Christian vision is that it not be exclusive of other traditions. Eastern and neo-Platonic mysticism are called upon for the elucidation of Christianity; for clarity of word and concept, tribute is paid to Greek philosophy; for the symbolic and mythopoeic imagination Mary Casey turns to the less rational elements of the Greek cosmos. There are numerous comparisons between Christ and Dionysus, and Epiphany is the conjunction of the two, in which we witness:

> the star
> showing Christ to the Gentiles
> the play of infant Dionysus
> with his father's lighting
> ('Epiphany II')

In 'Easter Day' Christ's first miracle is recalled:

> now is the child of the vine
> received new in the kingdom –
> . . .
> the fun of being Dionysus
> to turn water to wine

Christ is compared also to Adonis; John the Baptist is associated with Orpheus; and the meditation on the Transfiguration finds an astonishing, beautiful resolution in 'the vision of Eros'.

Beneath the Cross, the Virgin speaks, modulating from the gospel versions, with delicate evasion of controversy and provocation, into the voice of the earth-mother:

> now I am no more woman
> weeping and worn and old
> I am a copse in the spring
> my bones lithe hazel wands
> my breasts the tenderest buds
> ('Mary')

A sacramental faith neither fears nor shuns such inclusiveness; yet so widely ranging and encompassing an imagination as Mary Casey's is seldom to be found in religious poetry.

A properly sacramental religion makes for emotional wholesomeness, an absence of all sentimentality. There is no regret or lament at the Crucifixion or at the execution of John the Baptist: these poems celebrate ritual death, the event itself far transcended in the sacrament which it initiates. At the end of the sequence is one of the last poems which Mary Casey wrote, within days of her death. Each death is the breaking of a link, and there is no death so insignificant as not to break the chain; yet what is broken in death can be restored through suffering, personal and creative, put to the maintenance of the continuity of imagination:

> the undifferentiated suffering is energy
> to re-create the catena by heartbreak
> in art quartet four-line Greek epigram
> epistle unmake tradition

By death, each dying, the tradition of our Christ-bearing ancestors is broken over and again; and by suffering the catena is constantly made new. In such calm faith, in this extraordinarily tranquil poem, Mary Casey anticipated her own death.

The corruption of Christianity originated, and continues to originate, in a merely human response to death, and to the Crucifixion. Through her poems Mary Casey enables us to see, with clarity and precision, the symbols, rituals, sacraments, perpetually re-enacted, always renewed, by which our lives, and all creation, might be ordered. Lest that sound too easy, too innocent of pain and discord, Mary Casey insists that art and heartbreak are 'unlinked incompatibilities', but one instance of the inadequacy of the compromise sometimes taken for religion. Mary Casey's refusal of compromise carries most conviction in the nearness of death; to her end she persisted in her search for a genuine link, not necessarily in Christian art or doctrine; her poetry witnesses to a passionate intensity of looking, both within and beyond the Christian tradition, for a universal sacrament, a redeeming comprehension.

The last sequence, 'Geometrical Relationships', moves beyond the tentative framework of 'Christophoros'. Mary Casey's sacramental faith may be said to realise its own undoing, or unsaying, for these are poems occasioned by incidents and observations of life in Kenya, and almost stubbornly resistant to larger claims. Read independently of 'Christophoros' these poems might seem rather strange, for they are not descriptive poems about life in Africa, that take the exotic fauna and flora as poetic themes, or find in the naked violence of existence the occasion for an easy fable. The title of the sequence, 'Geometrical Relationships', indicates a degree of abstraction, a stance that is detached not out of fear or colonial aloofness, but the better to avoid the obvious, the stereotypes of writing about Africa.

It is obvious that the exotic is exotic, less obvious that it is still the task to measure the earth by ratio and proportion, by the numbers that alone can reconcile world and mind, earth and poetry. Mary Casey's project in this sequence is to engage in such a measure, by a most disciplined attention, while leaving implicit the metaphysical ground of measurement. A sacramental faith strives increasingly to realise value and significance in matter as matter, to appeal minimally to the transcendental. And what was given, as the circumstances of Mary Casey's life for some thirty years, was an extraordinary challenge to the faith of 'Christophoros'.

Most writing about Africa by settlers or explorers is content with difference, and assumes the pedagogic task of explaining difference. Few such writers have questioned the appropriateness of writing, or its purpose in the context of Africa. Those writings are always intended to be read by people living outside Africa, usually in the comfort of 'home'. What is odd and different is therefore offered in terms of explanation, translation, assimilation to the familiar. Writers such as Karen Blixen, Elspeth Huxley, Wilfred Thesiger – some of whom were known personally to Mary Casey – are celebrated for their gifts of communication: they are not known for their struggles with words and meanings.

Mary Casey had no interest in telling other people about life in Kenya; as we have seen, she had no interest in publishing any of her poems. Africa's challenge to Mary Casey is consonant with that of the visionary: how does one dare to utter, to write, to break confidence? Here, instead of addressing St. Paul's warning, Mary Casey concentrates not on divinity and its claims to secrecy, but on the sheer freak of writing. What Africa tells Mary Casey, as one of the main coordinates of her geometry, is that writing is odd, an affront, an absurdity. With a sufficient burden of culture and history, writing may appear to be natural. Yet, in Africa, poem after poem of Mary Casey's questions its right to be written, its presumption and vanity. Consider 'A Pair of Bushbuck':

> listen my heart's love
> there is not reason for poetry

or 'The Uninvited Noose':

> I don't want to write
> but black went the white

or, in a powerful revision of a familiar motif, 'For a Bird Dying on a Love-letter':

> where could I find healing
> for the torn bruised wing
> leg bent back and claw
> that no more could cling
> could love do this thing
> where her hand had been
> leaving the name of love
> of all birds' spring wooing
> there I laid bluewing
> still with unfallen head
> with sky-cutting tail spread
> with anguished weak breathing
>
> O by my soul you keep
> let the loved bird have life

But this bird, loved only by proximity to the word 'love' and the name of love, dies.

Although in matters of living and dying writing may not make anything happen, it is itself an event, an outcrop in Africa as it would not be in England. Such a rare growth is writing that it is actually the word, the poem, writing as such, that needs nurturing, far more than exotic birds or animals; for it is words that are truly out of place and vulnerable. There can be few poems explicitly prompted by the writing of a single, isolated word; in 'The Unseen Bird' the word's ordinariness dissolves in the radiance of its bird-like vulnerability:

> lightly love winged my word
> gaily I let the bird-
> blood in my leaf-green veins
> sing in the pen-pricked word
>
> 'shining' I writ the word
> air on a sudden stirred
> scared by the wings of love
> shadows of feathers whirred
>
> claws of the unseen bird
> curly hair lightly stirred
> pricked with the nails of love
> head bent to shining word

The contrast between 'shining' – a word itself bell-like and metallic – and all the soft rhymes on 'word' gives to this poem an aural landscape every bit as stark and physically 'there' as the expanses and horizons in Kenya. Yet the immeasurable, we might suppose 'incompatible', difference between the poem's 'occasion' and its setting is exactly what justifies the title: a visit or visitation by some creature entirely other, like the angel of the annunciation.

According to the pattern of the Word, words ought to be strange; and we should be vigilant in observing the oddity of words. It is at our peril that we domesticate words, and take them for granted. Here is the peculiarly happy juncture between Mary Casey as sojourner in Africa and Mary Casey as visionary. For both St. Paul and the reluctant colonial, the danger of writing is bound up with its power. And, properly grasped, any word will do. In 'The Unseen Bird' it is the act of writing that first puts 'shining' in quotation marks and then allows it to take its place as a shining word that draws the attention of love. It is writing that confers that transforming power, for good or evil; there need be no single, theologically charged, metaphysically laden Word that redeems, but any word, written.

Written, marked, scratched, scored. While writing may be out of place in Africa, a mark of European culture and colonialism, its fragility and oddity are not absolute. For writing is but one, if the most rarefied, of the sign systems by which humans find meanings in the landscape and the atmosphere, in the weather and the behaviour of animals, and by which animals learn of danger and of prey: 'we learn all their markings'. At the level of signs writing is only an extreme instance of the common task: markings bring together humans and animals in a common compulsion to interpret the earth. While the writing of words separates the human from the animal, bringing the human dangerously close to the divine, the reading of signs and marks binds the human to the rest of creation.

Just as Mary Casey's concern for a bird is matched by her attention to a word, so her reading of signs is matched by a claimed empathy with all those creatures subject to the biological compulsion to make and read signs. Empathising with the animals is, from Montaigne to Whitman, a trope and a gesture towards cosmic oneness: for Mary Casey it is what saves the word from aloofness and abstraction. Indeed, words are here not just the vehicle of the sacramental vision, but the very test of it: words must retain their materiality, the tangible sense of being marked and scratched in ground.

In the tally of the thrush's song Whitman found licence to carol his elegy for Lincoln, and Mary Casey finds in birdsong her most ready measure for the otherwise estranged craft of poetry. This is most obvious in the elegy for her uncle Will Powys, yet throughout these poems it is the birds, with rhythm and number in their singing, that afford an analogy, almost a home, to poetry and geometry. Birds not only sing like poets, but like poets they are readers of signs. One of the most remarkable of Mary Casey's poems about birds goes under the same title as a famous poem by Hopkins. Yet this 'Windhover' is not a real bird at all, but the image of one on a calendar – whose presence is so real that one might think the human observer had been decoyed:

> does he not turn his yellow eye
> as I do mine up to the sky
> June ended he will quit this place
> and I shall lose his still balance

This poem is a profoundly convoluted meditation on and measuring of signs, their distances and relationships from and with that to which they refer, or for which they substitute. This is a poem of geometrical intricacy, in which measuring is finally indistinguishable from that which is measured. Readers of the 'Christophoros' sequence will apprehend the sacramental significance of this, and they will appreciate the scope of Mary Casey's vision, and the challenge.

Another poem of complex daring, 'Speke's Weaver's Chantry', is in the extraordinary pacing of its syllables barely – yet triumphantly – a match for the 'twitter-wrought offertory nest' that it defiantly celebrates. And there is a commensurability – however negative – between the wondrous pointlessness of the bird's nest and the gratuitousness of poetry: the everlasting attempt to sustain one's existence amidst sheer wilderness. The value of Africa in Mary Casey's poetry is that there, without trappings or pretence, all creation is open to the awe of bewilderment. And that bewilderment is the disciplined state of the one who journeys on the *via negativa*, where there are signs but no destinations:

> on the way back to where there is nothing
> I am well content in the vesture of fog

'The Vesture of Fog' is a gloss on 'The Cloud of Unknowing', from whose author Mary Casey has taken her epigraph: 'in this unknowing knowing, well content to be nothing . . .' Beyond 'Christophoros' Mary Casey moves into the apophatic realm, where knowing is matched by unknowing, saying is answered by unsaying, and light and dark are barely told apart.

Charles Lock

MEDITATION FOR AVICENNA

'the epiphany of the Angel corresponds
to a certain moment and degree
in the individuation of the soul
when awakened to consciousness of being
a stranger
it becomes free of this world

The Bird
has the rank of a symbol
an image through which the soul
meditates on itself
and divines itself . . .'

                        after Henri Corbin

Full Circle

DAWN

the sky is like a shell
washed by moon-rocked seas
but darkness lingers still
caught among the trees

where close entangled boughs
will not let her go
O in this pure cold dawn
what might I not know

1944

FULL CIRCLE

where the hills make a home hollow
early emptied of the evening sun
the sheep come to rest with their riches
of pure grass built into golden fleeces
the old gray valley always lonely
feels the presence of this warm company

by the hut the shepherds come together
a thin smoke rises from their fire
on the no-colour of the hillside
their washed clothes hang along the fold
the scattered pattern of the flock waiting
night draws to full circle

Africa 1969

THE AEOLIAN BELL

long you grew black
on the cow's neck
swung and rung all day
in the folds of her dewlap
jangling and tolling to the swing
of great horned head grazing
only resting your clapper when down she lay
to dream to the roll of her cud

now you hang on your black leather thong
on the beam by my door
and close to my ear I hear
you faintly wind-tinkled
as if from afar on the hill

Africa 26.1.70

WINDY HILL

the sheep have gone away from Windy Hill
everywhere the grass grows long
lost the little paths they made from mound to mound
the cunning ways they found down the cliffs
between the rocks that barricade the valley

no smell of damp fleeces in the morning
no evening bleatings of the anxious ewes
whistlings and smoke from shepherds' hearths
please the solitary slopes no more only
untiring winds sing a thin sorrow

Africa 9.3.69

NESTS

this is my cobweb
moss tag-ends of grasses
with these I weave
an empty house
round with round door
a mid-June joy

the wren sped in
and by the small-meshed wire
guard of the church porch
out to the young sun
filled with the building
of her skilful dome

no home for freckled eggs
or nursling wrens and yet
a living work to fill
a waiting dusty space
so with tired mind I tuck
my childless happy verses
into the placeless crevices of thought

Mappowder church porch 15.6.71

THE POOL

all day by my door bowed
two black men break stones
a dull rhythm beats upon the sun

the shining drum drops behind the hills
the river gleams with another light
an arrowy wake

pursues the black duck
circling a single rock
this for her silent pleasure
in the shadow of the western hills

Africa 24.9.70

CUCKOO

cuckoo you call
from the far hill
again again
clear in the long day's rain
and years and hours
and hoarded minutes
all these mortal counts
are lost I only know
the cuckoo calls in rain
and love loves me again

23.7.71

THE SNIPE

this my most constant vision when I close
my eyes in sheltering palms
my mind's tired eyes
the snipe of narrow bill
and reedsharp cries
sprung into sullen air
from Acherusian swamps
and lost to view

                5.3.71

CUCKOO-CLOCK

for Mother

you go
so quiet
not quite tiptoe
in hope
with fear –
O will she come again
I here
I hear her call again –
pass through each open door
touch an unopened book
look
the clock stopped
the house of wood
within the house of stone
door shut
O bird
not even you at home

            Africa 31.7.70

NORTHWARDBOUND

swallows flying home
swallows call me home
sharp longing sharp blue-
winged air-cutting birds
bear off my heart for
home fearless without care
they fly low they go
feeding on their way
now by the sheep they play
a whirling gnat dance
over woolly backs
O best-loved of birds

now by the river
I watch day by day
pray for your coming
the first living blue
carefree air dweller
all the spring's promise
in one swift arrow
narrow-winged keen flight
swallow and river

Africa and England
22.1.67 and 28.3.67

A NIGHTBIRD'S CRY

my mind slipped down a nightbird's cry
and into darkness fell
a pool of darkness where I lie
bound by a magic spell

                1944

AFTER READING BASHO

a long gray evening
falling rain and grieving
at nightfall the dearest star
a most frail shining

                1968

'AS A SPARROW'

Saturn my morning star
and cold companion
with no conscious splendour
of bright compassionate shining
rises the timeless one
only the lonely in unsunned solitude
with lightless eye can look
into the heart's solitude

                12.5.68

CAPRICE

for three days and nights my mind was in darkness
no celestial ray pierced my brain
in Cimmerian gloom I lived and loved
this morning the moon turned my bed to snow
I looked into the face among smoky clouds
the moon looked into mine the gauze curtains drifted over
our ancient compact had been reaffirmed

                16.12.67

HEART BURIAL

O silence of love my both hands hold
when night comes and I lie alone
still now as the knight of stone
who holds silent in hands' fold
heart knowing all hearts' moan

                    12.5.68

EDEN

poets live in Paradoxes
and not always do not breathe
that breeze
the cool one
when day's done

                    July 1966

OUT OF THE GROUND

that odd kind of cold
warmer than golden sun-
beams stronger than
the heart's inmost desire
when that one is dead
and never answers
yet even in utmost absence
gone and buried
dead
is new life in the soul

                    20.7.71

FROST

frost with scriptural cold
writes all the moonlight night
moss and stone and hard high road
bear the traces white

grass and grief and bramble leaf
words are sharp with it
in a ring of icy weave
the lop-side moon does sit

on the wintry window glass
the texts are carven hard
frost the Torah frost Amos
hard frost in the heart

when across the turquoise sky
spreads the red of sun
cold of chiselled history
frost is all undone

            20–21.12.67

HOGMANAY EVE

dirge

now the months their wrappings worn
gather up with pensive hands
where the western pyres burn
cast them forth as the year ends

now the last dawn burns her stars
out across the gusty sky
and the winds that come from far
teach the quick dead leaves to play

love housels this winter day
night the phantoms draws to me
faces bent they go their way
yet each soul I well can see

in the clearness of the eyes
with their high impassioned light
learnt beyond the death of years
given speechless to my sight

            31.12.67

WATER-WHEEL

'the day of country milling is over'
the miller filling the doorway
the river up to his breast
geranium pot at his elbow
looks into nothing with the manifold
intensity of a lover who has mastered
the art of milling and knows
there is none to come after

this is not a pose
he stands at ease as do those
who ponder while the sack fills
and the chills of the river mingle
with the smell of hot barley meal
headier than pollen
while the leaning willows feel for
and finger the face of the river

and the voice of the mill is gone for ever
the organ heart of smooth water-power
throb and rumble of runner on bedstone
pick-dressed by candlelight clattering
teeth of steel in revolving pinion gnashing
polished crabapple cogs in the fly-wheel
the last miller stands still in his doorway
while   the   world   turns   over

                        27.10.73

(Written after looking at a copy of Gilbert Spencer's
The Miller painted in the years when I was a child at
the mill.)

DENNIS DAVIS

everyone is loved by someone
the gypsy fellow married to a man-
voiced bearded scold who scared
us children said in later years
when she was dead
he alone as he began
life a starveling reared on bread
alone bread's all right he said
but you want something with it

the black-haired woodland-bred
knacker kept a lone black mule
hard-hoofed old to draw his high-
wheeled cart we children feared
its creak the beat of mule's feet
along the muddy lanes we walked
in buttoned leather gaiters
we knew we'd see stiff legs sticking
over the sides of the cart maybe the head

of some old friendly horse dead
and Denny with his long whip
and long teeth and wild gypsy air
when he grew old and sick the grimed lines
deep grained in his cheek he came
to the mill Christmas-time and my father
had had a present a case of white wine
he brought Dennis in poured him glass
after glass and he drank to the years
of bread alone

22.3.69

CENTENARY

'the beautiful wild birds of unsolicited dreams'
                                    J.C.P.

this is the night I know
I am nothing of my own
long bones brown eyes
the scarlet tree of life
are no more mine
than is the child within

I am of those in the graves
with all the lives before me
in this mystery of ancestry
is it that I think
is it – Pindar and Corinna –
the breath of song

now when I would sing for those
whose blood commingled beats wild
in mine tonight
I tell only of Mary –
in the uninherited sky hear
the plover as they fly
cry one to the other
peewit   peewit

                    4.10.71

DIONYSUS

'Who gives to mortals abundance of life'

not bird-blood Dionysus
burns in my cool veins
curiously fusing creative elements
god of all that flows
imbruing my spirit
with life-fire of wine
untasted flaming
in dark soundless stronghold
of human brain

wild-waving hair of the god
breath of the vine
on the wind
in the lull after tender rain
rest and contentment of being
harsh the birds scream

15.10.70

FRESCO

stand silent a moment
let the Etruscan red
dancer before the dead
give you his word
his flesh flames with passion
his sky-blue and bordered *pharos*
is fluted to music
his head haloed with night
the tree's spiny twigs
his great hand thrusts at
bear nothing
under a row of heaven-blue hearts he dances
with that bird in the curve of his arm

silent you hear his word
you sad of soul
live as I the dancer
a bright adornment
to the light-hearted dead

17.10.70

AFTER THE STORM

I hold my hands a wimple for my eyes
that I may see the vision of the day
the egrets in the trees the six
white swan-white triangles in-
verted sails
the heaven washed new
and earth a paradise
diamonded in clear shining after rain

upon dazzling air they spread and preen and stroke
their silver wings
upon the cottage roof the thatch is dark
and in the open doorway stands
a straight green-mantled sunflower
with his head reaching the bristly
edges of the thatch

the sun has fled
the flowers bow their heads one to the other
the birds shake off the snowflakes from their wings

Africa 25.11.71

EDITH IN AFRICA

a small black-hooded bird of prey
lean as a single raven's feather
fingers ringed and diamonded
sapphire amethyst tourmaline
she climbed the shallow marble steps
with eager eye to the gallery
and the rings hung round her fingers' snow
and with her talons coraline
she scratched her poems in my brain
till all the cells grew red as fire
and hawthorn flowers softly came
and their round petals fell as rain
as summer's tears adown my cheeks
for all the love that's spent and gone
has left its sweets in the buds of May
and their stamens bright as the break of day
here in my creaking wicker tree
with whirr of wings and winnowing fans
and a hollow shell of black and gold
on elephant legs that knocks the rocks
I listen to the songs that drop –
as drops my heart through time –
from her green honeycomb and cherry rhyme

Africa 16.12.70

MOCKERY GAP

for Vera . . .

once this was the house of an elf-child
the little lady who kept frail life-hold
with her paints and dyed wool-balls
flowers by the walls and bird calls

I shall not open the door again
to find her alone with her loom
and a fire too low to burn too low to go out
the Russian toys and wings at the window-pane

was it this year she caught me with changeling hands
clung as a bat clings – darling I love you so
her cold eyes clear as pools of rain
in elf-land whence she came

. . . who died 29.10.67

Africa 5.11.67

THE RAINS BEGIN

for Sally

I want to tell how it is now
when together are trod under foot
horseshoe and crescent curled seed pods
with fluff balls of flowers
from the same tree they fall merge
into one soft underfold
become life-giving mould
with crisped leaves muted

as long thunder crackles
and woodpecker's patient tapping
wins from cloudgatherings dripping
rain sweeter to earth than liquid
honey and all is left denser and darker
after the storm has gone over
the tapping is patter from thatch
and honeydew sleeks the rails

open the windows wide to sun again
remember Sally how she loves the rain

Africa 15.10.70

FOR PETER

then springing through the door
for him always open
for the boy who called over
the ship's rails after farewell
'Up Above'
through the door held open
thirty years by that word
by the vision of youth
the man came
and from that meeting
glance connaissance embrace
until the too swift parting
the stronghold of arms
of full understanding
'Dear One'
at every and often meeting
of eyes the same the same the same
as before the ravaged generation
of life years

for he too broke
with his own hands amphoras
of love poured forth for all
love stored in their deeps
the passion only those know
who seek Him in the depths
drawing from broken jars
springs of living water –
was known in that reflection
of soul within soul
in the duplicate stars
community of mystery

26.7.67

UPANISHAD

for Cathy

Abishag had hair inveigling as in Indian
serenade tawny eyes as a young cheetah
named for the speckled nature of this
reflected consciousness that flickers
her profile in some of her variable
sunbird moods was grecian as
when her hair was drawn up in a
careless cusp for the bath

she came to cherish the coldness
the wounded spirit and oldness
to minister as a child alone can
to a distant sickness a present desolation
her reasonless hilarity her absences
in sultry sufferings saved meditation
from the invasion of sighs –
bare groves grow green to lips
responding to the philosopher's Eros
to small fingers divining with
stones and feathers the inquiring humility

I want to speak with you

Africa 23.3.72

WHO ARE AWARE . . .

for Edward Thomas with red poppies

the November rains begin with hesitation
whether to weep in grayness over all dead
all battlegrounds of the unhappy world
whether weeping would be seemly for the happy
thrice happy 'whom God
had doubled his spirit upon
and given a double soul unto
to be poets'
for they are the living the fiery word
when the battles are cold and out of mind

let fall your immemorial sorrows
for the anonymous dead November
the muffled drumming of measureless ancient rains
in days when love and death link chill
compliant fingers and I will hold
my heartless hand warm to my cheek
and praise the singers in war –
our 'one organic nature stretched to the full
both sense and soul in a sacramental sharing' –
who now in freedom walk the wide-wayed earth

12.11.72

TO ALYSE'S BROOCH

no need to kindle torches on Etna
to seek my jewel
the bright and sparkling stone
I have lost love-token keepsake
burning my breast with icy star rays
not though I wander through long nights
and dark-edged days
with head bent to the ground
and I am robbed for ever
of my loved stone's lustre
never could I need light
to seek a thing so bright

not for half the year
will the gods give you me again
but you will guide me with your shining
in the underworld
when I fall also to the darts of Artemis

Africa 9.3.71

TOPAZ

the sun in heaven
is my sole topaz now
and shines on me
although I am all dark
and return no answering fire
yet still I acknowledge
the philosophic Eros
and look with love on the earth
the spring sun shows me
on the lifted face and eyes
shining on a small bird
never still in wintry twigs
intent and finding the life it seeks

Africa 9.3.71

FOR CHARLES

there are those who move freely
through the doors of eternity
who stand with us visible invisible
who in entering take leave
leaving take nothing away

the reality of their being
is not the memory of boy
youth manhood shouldered
perhaps shouldered aside a little
giving the utmost because of
some unconscious denial
and holding in the deeps
that most precious of all wines
in close-sealed jars kept
for the longed-for Ithacan king

but none claimed the love draught
of the holy amphoras
and a night came
when a steady hand
broke with one stroke
the beautiful close-sealed jars
and the flaming wine
the red wine
was poured
a libation of life
to death

and with all that love shed
he walked light
through the door of childhood
into back into forward into
the ultimate liberality
eternity

12.7.67

FOR D.F.C

what can the poet do for the old dead
the head long snowed on with white hair
go to the burial or alone apart
pray

in that strait way
the grave
is room for rest
from labours of the day
in stillness lie the dead
in this long quiet
their well-being

there and here
keep silence of pure prayer

11.11.70

THE SLATE PENCIL

for Bridie

it is well when you are dead
to be remembered by the very old
by one who held the hand of the child
and was unafraid
of encountering with flying reins
when thoughts were wild
dark horses with jet-black manes

the sorrows the meaningless years
fall away from the heart of the old
you are a child again
and go with hand safe held
by the midnight water
the shining water staining
the stone with blood-red stains

now your eyes are closed
there is no more dark
for you but the old woman goes
grieving for you scratching
your name on distant stones
to the youth-giving music of memory

14.1.72

'HERZ MEIN HERZ'

love my love as you have learnt me
through my hands and feet and head
in the rush of unknown forces
running by me where I'm led

these are all innate and make me
the stormed and broken heart you know
never here and gone for ever
overrun and sure to take me
when their courses backward flow

O this haste is not confusion
if all elements are fire
how can there be state procession
in the rising of the sun
all is made and unmade through me
with an impulse not begun

when we stood two dark-eyed children
in the air so thick with pollen –
dust of the life-giving grain
sprinkled over all our senses
while the river sings before us
and our eyes are clear although our
days and nights spin far as stars are –
that one look taught all we needed
for our hands to bend the gyres

5.4.74

IN THIS ALONE

before this temple also of the spirit
is deserted
I will declare my faith for all who come after
who are as I am
in the abyss of pain
there is truth and the poet

Wyat Surrey Emily Brontë
Old English laments the bearers of ballads
Homer and Pindar and Sappho
who touch gold in the living vein
in this dazzling sorrow
hold hands
in this Alone
there is a fellowship

now let the coping fall
the columns crack
the votive lamp go out
when all is given
no need of altar stone
or inmost shrine

5.11.70

HELIOS AND HADES

although there is no poetry my deare
I can make for you from my hoard of words
yet you have built a nest of singing birds
where silence was and all day long I hear
a song of appleboughs although the year
cries winter and we go down the long dark
together by the well-known twilight road
where no birds sing and our young suns are cold

but there are branches touching where the thrushes
will sing us into night will you remember
how it was once and how he turned quick head
before the frosts began before December
when hearing that clear singing of the thrushes
we said new suns will shine among the dead

12.1.68

THE SCARLET SWAN

'moyst with one drop of thy blood my dry soule'

fearless as the shining of the river
is your soul's shining
this is the clear vision
and all within you shines

the wooden footbridge waiting
here and not here
a simple preparation
a means of crossing
the vision's intolerable brilliance

after we have gone over
not hand in hand but flowing
we see through the green mead
gliding on unseen water swan
wings arching heart's consummation

      18.4.69

REMEMBRANCE

'and thus gat oblivion of toils that were bravely borne'

O you cannot remember
that is worst of all
for all day long
the long day
my heart talks with you
in visions you living
warm withdrawn
under the mask of whiteness
the clarity of eyes deceiving
intangible incandescence

remembrance is a frailty of the living
a necessity of here being broken
there no need of fragments
not the most brilliant
samples of light-shattering mosaic
because you have drunk Lethe
I cannot forget to remember
I can only gather together
shed feathers papers
minutely writ in that Greek script

make with green leaves limpid libations of water
my offerings to the dead

                                                    20.10.70

TO – IN AFRICA

the call of hearts that know but do not meet
is too lovely a pain to be cancelled by holding hands
by two heads bent to the same page
talk of a poem that white rift
in a tempest torn by the narrowest horn
of gold of a day old moon seen
together to remember
or a memory a thin crescent
seen that day on Lesbos
over the young Aegean sea

                                                  28.7.68

TO A SILVER LOCKET

the heart has phases as the moon
but only once shines full

                        15.5.68

'ARE THOSE YOUR TEARS'

must I drink Lethe and forget the stars
irradiant exaltations of the night
each in communion with the heart of light
that they may burn a way clear through my death
they will not lose their shining in that stream
and from the long dark bank my eyes give joy
to my most inward soul which will not die
because there is no Lethe for the stars

when you bend down my love to drink the river
that curves round all our life then let your eyes
find burning there the unforgetting stars
and if oblivion takes away all else
now when our souls are drinking one the other
we with the stars are free of that cold river

                                      31.8.67

VINTAGE

the earth settled comfortably
round the vial they planted last November
prays for no further disturbance
in its intricate tasks of consuming
and consummating death

but men have a longing for soil
made sacred by ashes
and corpses rotted to mould
they will dig here again
uproot the violets

on a morning of early spring
when birds sing Valentines
and rooks for all the cold
pull sticks the light will find
some trace of white impatient dust

17.7.70

LOST

last night I lost Mary
where are you
the known intensities of reading
the life-giving stream I have not betrayed
of the poet to drink of another
I called them within me
no answer
where are you

snare hung from tree
where airs cool noon
twisted wires stout pegs
hit into earth
that preparation for death
for a wild gazelle
reminded me
this your last day

in the former November
the kingdom of human consciousness
none other can know
was dismantled for ever my love

Africa 5.9.70

'WHEN YOU LOOK AT ME...'

I

'for the living know that they shall die
but the dead know not anything'
because of this thoughts gather
assemble round the dead to be
words form a sweet song as we bend
over our own selves dead

for alive we look upon our outspread hands
know head and ruffly hair
and eyes astare upon the mystery
that these will still be there
and we who thought they were us gone –
for evermore
how can this thing be

how can this song of yours for your own death
speak living words into my heart
my love which you alive spoke only when you looked
on yourself dead – surely because
this wild strange heart of one alive
lives for you are there

II

'when you look at me after I have died
and note the tidy hair, the sleeping head
closed eyes and quiet hands – do not decide
too readily that I was so. Instead
look at your own heart while you may and see
how wild and strange a thing a live man is and so
remember me'

always your mood is the imperative
alive and dead, in heaven as on earth
this time I do obey in full content
and look where all the room is warm with you –
the living know that they shall die
the dead know everything

21.11.70

O GIVE TO MY BONES

O give to my bones the honour of fire
not the cold earth
this is the swift renewal
liberation from heavy flesh
into thin flame of spirit
the nature of dry mind
fire

O earth earth earth earth
life-giving
charnel house of flesh
I praise you in clay

now the white ash flies
calcium crumbles
the immortal fires
children of love
singing and burning in the veins
brain's wild-fire
free

                    24.8.69

SUNT LACRIMAE RERUM

it is the things make ache the heart
the sparrow with a broken wing
brushes the soul with woe
that soon must go
but the chosen things
handled and mended and smoothed with love
the feather in a drawer
the jewelled things
rosewood and satin and cedar
books each one known and in its own place alone
who can bear these
not for all Milarepa's rhyme
can love brave these

                    26.8.69

PIERIAN

I have no fears that I may cease to be
my mind the quiet over all things draws
of being no more when the last passion's past
but I could fear the grace that's given me
of poetry the energy of love
and sole intensity of solitude
may cease to bring me to the troubled spring
which lets me sing my love before I die

                              14.9.69

RESTORATION

this is my will
that in the hour of death
I do lie still
and in this very quiet
body's quittance
foreknow the grave

and with no fear my mind
gathers the treasures my heart once loved well
each one marked known –
for they are mine alone –
surrendered
with this grace

that love has given them
I cannot tell them over any more
but all that made the interchange so fair
is with me still and clear
as one by one they go
and I lie last alone

                              7.10.69

AFTER A READING OF *EAST COKER*

perceiving
the poet is aware of a double immediacy
the instant surprised – that it should be so
could not be otherwise
and as well for the poet who is seer
(things invisible to see)
it was known before that it should be so

this is involuntary
surely he would rather
be unaware of perceiving
receiving simply the image
mute attentive that will not be again
because I do not hope –
that is a lie

it is at a certain intensity –
loss of succession in time –
one sees as a god would
visions of men without human background
toil dread horror of ageing bodies
imperatives of flesh
the stone walls

that have eaten centuries of sunlight
drunk immemorial rains
they have this immediacy of prophecy
and the face of the old

11.10.69

NOT AFTER PLUTARCH

'Comfort me with apples'

parallel lives of one mind in two climes
this is my present reality –
beginning with rivers running reflective water
with wind nearest comparison of spirit
and apple orchards of forgotten tribes
fruit trees grown gaunt and tall
the apples small tough-skinned as berries
rough but tendersweet to teeth
used to crack hazel nuts or the long-sheathed filbert

this from the equator is the far isle
of the blest the happiest immortal hyperboreans
now I am sure this haunting of apple-eating
and gathering long painted ladders baskets
and measures heaped up grass lumpy
with tumbled harvest is the childhood be-
ginning of the discovery of Avalon
where the sun sets and all those western clouds
and shadowy hills are stained with human dreams

forget the fright of Eden deep is the Vale
of Avalon with sleep and mellow apple fruitage

                                          2.8.70

FROM WHOM NO SECRETS ARE HID

from whom no secrets are hid –
this inmost heart is free
fearless because of this
the shadows are of summer –
foliaged trees above an eastern facing slope
that throw their blue-green dark
down that gray steep
when the sun moves evenwards
and these shadows contemplations
reflections in the sheer hillside
as in perpendicular still water
correspond to the inmost recesses
of the heart imaging
love recognised because even the secrets
of love are not hid
although the sunshine is dark
over the buttercup meadows
O my love

Trinity Sunday 1.6.69

WHEN AFTER THE COLD

when after the cold
there is a recovery of irradiance
and Athene sheds again grandeur
on head and shoulders
the god remembers his shining
and fire devours the bones
this is re-entry into the mystery
of integration
through disintegration
of the electric particles of being
the force that holds whirls
the stars of frosty October
races through the fingers
that trace not love
but the quiet brow of thought

                8.6.69

THE RUSTLE

lay yourself down
wrists on hips
hands in groins
straight as monk
on rigid bed
first brief sleep
death divine
body cast off cries –
do you want me darling

no breathes soul
this your departure
is my absolving
you wake in alarm
from freedom of care
let yourself rest
in this absence of dutiful light
now my wings unfold –
I will come back with day

                14.6.69

'HE BROUGHT ME
TO THE HOUSE OF WINE'

see how still the wine jars stand
waiting for their lord to come –
once they all stood stiffly sealed
tight caps set with wax
the dark drink stored within
fireless cold and dead

on a day love's eyes looked through
clear into the soul
and the round-mouthed
smooth stone jars
since that day have stood
open with the flaming wine
red for all who will to see

no one tastes
no cup is drawn
still the jars stand full
without cobweb
without dust
bright the wine and new

                7.5.70

MAUD

why do they sing so
what makes them do it
the old lady said
and blackbird and thrush
the thunder gone over the rush
of wild rain on the window-pane
they began it again again strain upon strain
with commingling notes
with silver and gold throats

what's the use was the thought
behind her words –
had she never known
the agony of energy
pent in the soul
without communion
not all this my dear
can be 'used' in prayer
in silence in commerce
with living and dying
poetry and suffering run into singing
joy into singing singing singing
my feathered birds

8.5.70

AT THE WINDOW

for Eleanor

a feast to the eye
this bullfinch close by
black velvet cap
slaty gray back
rump white as the snow
all sparkling below

the sunset bright stain
on his breast it is plain
he seeks to repair
on my Japanese pear
for the buds that he eats
would be red as pomegranates

flame-flaunting flowers
in April's fresh showers
were they not within him
now the bush must be dim
and my shy Muse retires
deprived of her fires

while Goethe's gives *him*
in one gulp at all hours
birds buds fruits and flowers
and the theory of colours

      29.12.76

ODYSSEY

for those who drink in silence
salt tears
it is forbidden to mourn
the tears Odysseus shed
he swallowed lost in the waste of waves
when the wine-dark sea
was bitter brine for him

he mourned aloud
and voyaging found home
but stranger seas
a wilder landfall called
nor could the rooted bed of olive wood
hold the gray rover
Penelope

has no grave mound
to heap for him
no gathering of stones
and all the seas of her false lover's sailing
are not so salt as those that rock her soul
are not so tempest-torn
as her heart's silence

                18.7.70

PHLEGETHON

my ambition outflares Dolon's
who sought to handle Achilles'
immortal horses
for one day I thought
if I could make a song
as clear as Orpheus sang
in the heart of Persephone
I might stand living
close by the tall black poplar

this is the utmost penalty
to have learnt in drinking love
there is no Lethe

                10.11.71

A JOURNEY INTO WALES

for Gerard

I

pèlerin

every journey must have a chorus
renewal by repetition
a musical motif insistent
now near now distant
for fear the wayfarer wearies
attention drifts sense dozes
the wheels are no longer Ezekiel's

for this journey into Wales
the chorus is wrens
one song many iterant singers
all the way to the mountains
wherever the itinerant tires
the face of the eagle is recalled
by the shrilling with its impudent curlicue

the choric wrens' opportunity
is the summer silence of birds
the dark woods overhang
recession after solstice
obliviousness (for the journey is endless)
shivered into seer's astonishment
by tremolos from invisible wrens

II

Ffestiniog

agate-eyed sheep do not sleep
akin in this to the Lord of hosts
their Keeper Whose ways not theirs they consider
as they move upon the mountains
go into green alcoves in the hills
rub shorn ribs against rocks
rest ruminant upon rocks

as the Lord they rest as the spirit of the Lord they move
and breathe upon the mountains
according to their nature sheep and their Maker
sabbatise without sleep by night in stars
that touch their heads solitary sheep bleat
and distance answers the dark-eyed lamb of God

July 1976

TAO

open the door to the timeless
you will be engulfed
look into the grass-roofed room
the door is wide open
there is quiet
nothing moves in its place
is he who lodges here near
has he gone to the mountain
have his feet taken him
so far away
he will not return

wait while your heart bids
no matter if he does not come
in absence you receive the essence
man's nature remains in his sojourning place
when door and window open on the void

Africa, at Springs Cottage 22.11.75

COMPOSURE

mesembrial utterance
I am willing to wait for
until the lifelong day
my firmset earth
dissolves clear away
here is all May
undulant unhurried
comprised by this lovecroon the dove
slender silent-winged
immemorial turtle

inarticulate compassion
May madness swifts' screams
spring surges halting sorrows
all that can never be said
becomes the parched mouth of the dead
until in a distant once touched on
unknown abode
the turtle dove pauses muses
most tranquilly composes
her unalterable language

                        23.5.75

ON MISSING PLOTINUS

'this is of the greatest power
to be able
even in evils to find meaning
for things grown shapeless
to find forms transformed
to be enough for this – '

I read very early
in the hush of day
lilacs leaning to the window
mingling faint breaths with my longing
for Plotinus living –
for while I was writing
he was living within me
interpenetrating intellect
in poetry of creating

reading these his words
on Providence
at the distance of a stranger
I caught his tones
within an illuminated emptiness
was this desolation
recession of lilacs
the Meadow of Truth

O listen this thrush singing

24.5.69

'JUST AT DAWN'

not many are the women
for whom the experience of their mode of being
is alive in the creative mind of man
the writers who touch this note
have passed beyond the scope of tenderness
known in the nature of mortal men and gods
there is no desire no eros
no ideal romance no words poetical
instead a breathing quiet infused with intellect
that is not of man – boy or girl – or of dog
this quality is not amenable to the cosmos
as generator of physical elements
nor has it commerce with worship
which is the simplest most total emotion

shall I say I compare this living woman
her being in the genius of man
with a piece of jade
innocent not because it is uncarved
but because after submitting to all workmanship
and impressions of the craftsman
there is perfect reversal –
pensiveness laughter hands
that wave and clasp are connaissance
that acts without action

10.4.74

SIRAKOI

for W.E.P.

the air is sweet from the desert
arrive unpack escape
from the range of voices
listen –
now I lie in a den
the toppled tree *imogen*
a maze of serpentine
intertwined twigs
tangled trunk creeper-hung

listen the thin wind sings a seasong
deceiving
there are twitterers and cicadas
the land is haunted
ghosts in the stones
that cairn a grave
long before Masai came
and went leaving the name
Sirakoi – Zebra Water

the wind sang the same –
Orpheus of grass and bush –
before men from the Nile came
before strangers heaped boulders
to leave a mark
for those who come after
sang in the conched ears
polished and heedless
of the stone-workers

pear-shaped hand-axes
hewn by hands human then
of those we call stone-age men
strewn on the cracked ground
the same wind is clean and new
sweetness of haunted loneliness
listen
a rough breathing drinking in singing wind
Moss has found me

Africa 14.1.70

Note: Moss – a Border Collie

URCHIN

owl far away
sky bare of stars
Saturn with sullen eye
unshining light
heading for exile
alone
turn to the dark wall

turn a fading ray
groundwards
creature with dull eye
still at my feet
touch with living hand
finger gently thorns
go in peace

           23.10.71

Christophoros

PART ONE

CHRISTOPHOROS

God giving himself incarnate
to immolation
is the root being of all men
who fall into the hands of the living God
who bear not only the bare cross of wood
a stake but bear also the burdened rood
who by day by night
go down to Hades
wearily how wearily climb again to light
we castaways on the coasts of light

MEDITATION

on reading the Old Testament

is it the Promise implicit
or poetry kindled in the deepest dark
the furthest reach of the heart
by prophet and seer sweet singer
of Hebrew song David and David's son
Solomon of the Song of Songs

but the soul is readily persuaded
to believe in the high-winged joys
thy youth shall be renewed as the eagle's
the consolation after the draught of tears
the dissolving of worm-gnawn bones
sorrow and sighing shall flee away

and those threats on the heads of our foes
the setters of snares who privily lie in wait
to smite devour ruin our best desire
those broken teeth and jawbones are passed over
in keeping maybe with the moods of men
but without part in the ultimate mood of God

MY SON

on the other hand it may be the concrete simplicity
of these threats of destruction
that gives them their unreality
for in inmost sensitivity in
the source of nerve-quivering life
the soul knows one string only and
this vibrates to   is tragedy

on this not poetry itself can redeem suffering
not the words of the Saviour
all else is wrappings and lendings
thought and beauty and gatherings of flowers
pure passion the quiet graces of living
are disguises and pretty devices
to cover cruelty and self-crucifixion

NOTHING IS WITHOUT A PART IN SOUL

rhythm is proportion
progress of pilgrim hours
advance to prepared attainment
a journey for the feet

the stranger's journey is not for the feet
he comes with the air
is where the trees were
beggar in wrap too limp to flutter
while the shufflers the footsore pilgrims
move pass by place and replace
their ingrained souls
and dust is spent on his face

the stranger is Ariel and Caliban
thoughtless winged heel
too hollow with hunger to feel
the ground those feet thud
and scrape over drum and fiddle
there must be goal and occupation trail
otherwise pilgrims are only refugees
the stranger is none of these

these dispossessed who seek a country
advance on their human feet and wave a hand

MOSES

I

'the voice of the Lord makes the wilderness quake'

I am the man Moses
called from the life-giving river
the papyrus crib adrift on the waters
to lead the children of Israel
man of God to my death day
where now I take my stand
the red sun founders on the promised land
dread as the burning bush that seared
my raging soul with vision of the Lord
the voice of Israel's God that night and day
sounds down the gorges in this savage mountain
this ground is holy

out of a basket daubed with slime
the wealth of timeless Aegyptus
he plucked me to track the wilderness of Zin
alone in the famished desert
nameless to keep my father's sheep on Horeb
terrible to compel the tribes by tribulation
where for their tread the law no smooth way laid
no rest with the vortex of dust
the consuming fire of our God
Lord God give this last vision to my eyes
cracked to the quick by fire and furnace suns
to feel from the grave's edge Thy heritage

II

the bearded lion

they say my sight is keen
because I see with visionary eye
not the promised land of Jehovah
I feign to extend my look over
graved with features of clear meaning
imperishable as the tables of Torah
I am now of a different mind

listen young man
Moses the mouthpiece of God
is absconded of all my mighty speeches
I have less recollection than this thicket of thorns
my aged beard has of the hairs
the desert winds strung and
sang through and sparked off with sand
this body where the ecstasy of life-withdrawal
is annulling and fiery as my loveplay with Zipporah
contains more mystery
than the literature the scribes will use me for
take care none finds the carcase
when the lion is dead and gone
this people is one for tombs empty or full

III

'the spirit of wisdom'

'find me a cleft in the rock for sepulchre
no cause for them to mourn a man
who living beheld Jah the Lord of life'
then Moses covered with his two palms
his calculating eyes and bowed himself

and the young man who stood by firm
on his feet while the mountain shook
and his spirit groaned within understood
the last commandment of him
whom the Lord knew face to face

WILDERNESS

I

here where the land is scorched
with torrid sun grass is frost-
hoared starched bleached by white heat
of zenithal rays' beat
only towards day's end
light-shivered thoughts bend
to the brink of earth's dark
brass sun bends to stark
ridges of granite fells
and arctic blue light wells
into the argent grass
indigo shades in harsh
mountain and pyramid
uncover gulfs day hid
mind to a dryness wrought
'thought thinking upon thought'

II

from the pyre

land dry as the high-
praised mind of Heraclitus
scares us
rondures of rocks
jawbones dust and thirst
and the brazen sky

yet red flowers rise
and blue and gold
and white among these stones
jagged as dog's teeth
and birds of paradise
fly through the cruel thorns

this very day Good Friday
one unearthly green cool-
burning in desert's furnace
with lustre of high heaven
and day's great star
never before I saw
this Phoenix

III

exiled

you can give your soul
the whole of your dry mind
the most sensitive responses
of love of landscape
to Africa you give all
to a barren beauty
why the swift rivers
springs groves trees
and wildernesses
the high-flying birds
are an unreciprocal emptiness
decorations on a suffering consciousness
that flinches wishing to be numb
cannot be understood

only as time passes the pain
the scars the burnt-in woes
are beyond the succour of rain
the blackbird sings the thrush
the ringdove coos again
they call me my heart has forgotten
the mediaeval answer

IV

one prays

riga quod est aridum

leprosy the white sickness
the sin against the sun
is sun-engendered
in this seared land
what is left is skeletal
bone-white in the white death
grass ground down pulverised
standing stark stalks
brittle as insects' wings
as infants' stiff finger-twigs

into the brazen heaven
from arid ridges lift
snowy sails billowing
airy carefree craft
adrift in their thirsty sea
of mockery blue
with slower steps day by day
the starven cattle stray
lie still in the blaze of moonwhite nights
and do not rise again in the bright the golden dawn
no frosty sparkle on these sun-frozen plains
only the emerald dove in the grove remembers the rains

V

El Khalil

three red round flowers
through the trees
see
shall I not go alone as far as these

where I stand to pray
the shade of this tree
makes dark as I sway
full light of the sun
behold

go down into the earth
cold the cave
within the dull clay
stay
matrix and tomb
for man

look
on the side of the hill
the tree divided
strain of wrought limbs
feel
rough and dry this wood

(they call this Friday Good)
noon
drive home the point
nails hold the high sun
spear
three flowers of red

the hour is passed
wait
these angry thorns
thrust
my head edged with pain
wait for the cry

VI

Northern Frontier

then there is the thornbush desert's
spiny hot monotony
redbrick ground without the pattern of courses
gray as foot-weary pavements
bone-white to add needles to eye smart
these changes of soil in stages of ten miles or twenty

tindery trees grow up crumble to dust
return to the wind spirit cries out
for the works of man the burial ring replies
thorns hacked and spliced in a cheval-de-frise
that desert instead of hyenas
be fed with shrivelled corpses

but the barricade soon corrupts
ants eat the slats stuck up for pillars
knelling of wooden bells on twiny necks
knocks dully over as lofty cleft-lipped
contemptuous heads drift by shuffle feet
shifting the ash where someone lit a fire

and went away for ever lost almost before they are seen
in the arid mock orchard *vaguli cameli*
Somali with pickled skins and pickaninnies
but thornbush has waymarks for them

VII

encyclical

the soul is a clear call
through all the uproar
screaming of gulls
above storm-wrecked hearts
gnashing of teeth
of cogwheels
men bound to the wheels
that turn without mercy
until by that rote they learn
they say
there is no mercy
turn turn turn
wheels of work
turn in their turn
wheels of rebirth

who in the multiplicity
of intricately interplying
evolutionary wheels
heard of pity
amid wheels and wails and uproar
the piercing call is silence

THE BAPTIST

I

'most musical reed'

the young girl's dancing
the oath   her childlike asking
what shall I choose
her fateful obedience
to the hate of another
her rhyming feet in reckless return –
the narrow sandals flash
in the dark palace corridors
practising the skill of her dance

every mythology must have
a severed head
that it may not grow old
but bodiless sing the oracles of God –
Orpheus down the eddying river
the head on a charger
carried by the dancer
these two have spoken
hail one the other with cold mouths

John saw ever the soft-feathered bird
upon the head of God
Orpheus' wind-swift fingers
enticed sparrows after him to Hades
prophet and lyrist live by wild honey

II

'and the voice said Cry'

nature poetry and hermit poetry
this I read of Ireland
nothing of the history of ideas
and my midsummer mind
haunted by John Baptist
called as I closed that book of Keltic green
he came up from his wilderness
with cold wind crying
through the Gospel
the freedom of solitude
with long hair and words
knife-edged as reeds
cut hands staining the river
he dashed on their heads

head-hunters these Kelts
heads on posts on pillars
may be without ideas
but the dancing girl
the head on a platter
will outcry Plato

III

'led by the spirit'

the voice of one crying in the wilderness
my heart says
I want no cry
this is my gentle desolation
my Wilderness of Zin
where sin has no origin
and there is no redemption
in these secret sands
the dry rocks shine
with my dry brain
the sharp mountains
biting bare sky
know no sacred
law-giver's footfall
silence of desert
my silence
of owl death-winged
my banished bird
in the cowl of night

and the voice said what shall I cry
I reply
my heart wants no cry
in solitariness
in savage desolation
there is no cry
and there is no redemption
but the wilderness crying
out of my dry heart
crying Christ
delivers my desolate solitariness
and I know the soul of Man
crying Christ

IV

arul

my spirit
a reed shaken with the wind
bends with intensity of wavering
between John of midsummer
more than a prophet
and midwinter John
who pronounced the word of light

cry cry cry
in the wilderness of light
in the dread divine of long night
I waver and cringe and writhe
with John of Merlin
with John of the Ecstasie negotiate
my spirit cries what shall I cry

witness of all things is the spirit
visible in the inclining whispering
reeds as they rustle and shiver
a wavering in absolute consciousness

arul: reception of grace, change of consciousness

ANNUNCIATION

*'my presence shall go with thee
and I will give thee rest'*

because the child's heart is single
one voice speaks first the Word
into the ear unaware
and the echo continues clear
through every afteryear
when all grows elaborate
and layer is built into layer

alone with desire to know again
the kingdom of heaven given
into the heart of a child
I listen and wait and hear
the word of John son of thunder
the lamb which takes away the sin of the world

Mary of Nazareth

this is the miracle
that virginity given of God
can only be broken by man –
now I am alone among my companions
for that I stand tall and narrow
my robe straight and neat about my cool round knees
my girdle clasped as usual by my own fingers

how can this thing be in my young spring
when anemones spill over the rocky hill
incarnadine
it is the nature of girls to bewail their virginity
whether or no –
for me all I know
since the shining wings overshadowed me
the light of his countenance stilled my fear
is the birth of song in my soul

O my beloved is the young roe
he leaps upon the mountains of Bether
he feeds among the lilies
my musings are become his pastures my eyes are upon him
with clear shining after rain

'I did but taste'

all secrets of my inmost heart are free
for love to see
my hand will tell
if my tongue cannot of the silent well
where the clear waters flow
in darkness of the soul

my love you are the haunted wood
from which they carved the rood
where all the trees
drip honey sweeter than the work of bees
in the forbidden dew I dip my rod
my eyes enlightened see the living God

(I Sam. xiv. 27 and 43)

'a sword shall pierce'

now the first month of this new year
is going as the full moon
begins her waning
and Hannah prays again
her lips moving
that she may learn childbearing
and the old priest hearing
prays for her supplication
that it may find fulfilment

so the older Hebrew and Mary
who grows not old
who is always the innocent child
of the gentle conception
bends with her lips unmoving
upon birth and death
pondering in her heart
learning in sorrow
how the soul is enlarged

Gabriel

Gabriel
stands before the young girl
the angels and archangels
know not evil and death
they appear as the shining forth
of celestial space
the falling away of bonds
flesh transfigured

angelus Dei nuntiavit Mariae

BIRTH

man in his woe and grief
seeks for the beasts
those which in meekness bear
burdens of man

in their large company
hushed is his grief
just as the grass they graze
thistle and rush

grasping the dark wood
of the worn manger
wait while the body breaks
in primal creation

now when the hour is past
hear the first cry of life
in the long winter night
God's word is spoken

EPIPHANY

I

come to light

lode-star

the music of epiphany is stillness
the unbreathing depths of nature
before the storm of terror
revelation lightnings
instantaneous realisation
by the unprepared of the unknown

the god is shown in light
uncreate
intensity of vision
fulfilment with no toil
no labour of hands
the shining flower the star

this the conjunction of Christ
and Dionysus the looser-of-care
here we behold with those immortal eyes
now deity runs from east to west
as lightning the earthbound face
there is no refuge
eternity

II

star-struck

the difficulty of epiphany is
that what we are given
the star
showing Christ to the Gentiles
the play of infant Dionysus
with his father's lightning
is so much more than action
human doing even the acts of apostles
that we are stricken in mind
forget that for vine and grain
there must be labours and pain

that consciousness is known
'as a spiritual activity of thinking'

in heaven light runs through light
for my philosopher – on earth the poet
is rare who can take a star
before our dense air darkens
that flaming hair

III

'unsearchable riches'

star-led

how do we know we are wise
we look in each other's eyes
and see the tiny flames
at our nightly bivouac fires

the star we saw in the east
points us towards the west
we the perennial sages
observers of celestial harmonies
for the birth of a new song

we know light has no tongue
speechless we dint the sands
until the dawn when we reach
the Word shown before by the star
for the last time lift our gifts

to the backs of our kneeling beasts
we recognise by our gold and frankincense
and bitter myrrh that we are wise

because where the star has led us to open our treasures
they are less than nothing before
the young girl and her child in the stall

IV

epilogue for epiphany following three meditations

after sleep and the warning dream
we turn our serpent-necked camels
to the east steering them another way
by the high constellations which change not
the animals on the homeward journey and unladen
are not unwilling no call for the goad
but for ourselves it is not so
we talk to forget the splendour and leader
the shining of our former companion

why must it be that fulfilment
is like wind in the hand
even for the wise in ancient learning
the king returning to his own land

only when the morning star rises before us
and jewels on turbans and harness sparkle
dimly we look in each other's eyes and say –
we gave our treasure and adoration
these will be remembered in the new song
with the star
the star we saw in the east

MEDITATION OF ST. JOSEPH

I am glad I bought that blue robe for our bridal
since I have been standing here in the stable
these days with cobwebs catching my hood
watching her nursing the child
her head bent to him when he shines in the straw
where he lies in the crib
and the ass's breath is on him
the cattle's deep breathing
I have learnt many things

if the others saw God as she sees Him
the pure in heart
they would never look any otherwhere
as these creatures see Him and do not move away
the shepherds who came the first midnight
with wonder with rough faces reflecting glory
they looked and went away
and others whose lids lifted once and fell again

this my meditation and marvelling
shows that I also in learning many things
have not learnt Him
those strangers and high-crowned kings
who told of a distant star
and made mystic offerings
they also prayed to the babe and went their way
but she abides simply in folds of blue holds
this child who is our near and morning star

SNOWSTORM

mountain mind find together
chasm in the heart of whirling cloud
driving with unattainable mystery
with terror of fathomless abysses
lo a horror of great darkness
in cloven granite cradles
nurses the uttermost whiteness
from chaos out of the void
despairing of form exquisite
crystalline ice down of white
swan on lips
dandelion aloft adrift
in the Gate of the Mists
heart mountain together know
how falls sorrow's pall
wait day's end believe
glory of nightfall
behold from heart jagged from
unageing crags
rest death's muffling pall
mountain with cloven peak
heart's soul high shining
with snow unattainable
attend the splendid night
the epiphany of stars

TRANSFIGURATION

I

'the light which lighteth every man'

on the eve of the transfiguration
meditation on light
first and best symbol
so clear the dark air is invisible
a star marks the birth
the lightning flash of Zeus
the uncreate light of Tabor
and that self-shining shrine
of Dionysus on Parnassus
child and god of the Muses
together fulfil the promise
the divine dark of love
the dark of betrayal
and it was night
are overcome on these high mountains
where clouds come to sleep
to shelter this mystic irradiance
the vision of Eros

II

Christ irradiant

among such various and strange transmutations
why may not Nature change bodies into light
and light into bodies?

everything shines there

the quanta of energy pass into vibrations of light

today we consider   we face the vision
the best Plotinian symbol
mediated   that our eyes may not dazzle
through the countenance and apparel
of the man on the mountaintop
Christ irradiant
the many-coloured raiment white with
the flesh of the god shining through the seamless garment

the light uncreate of Tabor
kindles the altar candles
the planetary mosaic eye of my
flame-adoring midnight moth
my mind's eye musing

when someone no longer adores on the mountain
or at Jerusalem the hour has at last come when
he has become a son and adores the father in freedom

'FOR THE WATER
OF THE WELL OF BETHLEHEM'

the sweet psalmist of Israel for water
himself asks a wounded spirit who can bear
is the word of his son
and even though forgive forget
be given the soul
the most inward dweller
the stripes are unhealed

by them the familiar
has never been before
to stand in the open door
rush forward bow strained to the full
withdraw
the arrows in quiet restore
to the heart the inward quiver

build precariously over the wounds
Prince Andrew's edifice of needles
and shavings frame with these hands
the painted ikons
wounds and stripes are before
the creation
in man's sense of the words

they are newness of life the water
is the blood of men

MAUNDY

here are all the symbols
of a simple state
water basin towel
row of sandalled feet

now the feast is over
garments laid aside
ready for the torments
what is there to hide

now the pleasant walking
over holy ground
speech and sweet communion
these their end have found

best is voice of water
blessing feet and soul
and the small hoofs' clatter
of the ass's foal

here the state of manhood
has no more to do
kneel with head bowed over
it is left to you

GOOD FRIDAY

all day darkness
was over the land
at nightfall
the black cypress tree
at the end of the garden
which may mark the tomb
points to the yellow illumination
of the much-worshipped moon

'him of the tree'

I am the life of the tree
cool ichor secret juice
stealing sharper more potent than dew
within my rugged sheath upwards
spreading abroad in arms
in tentative fingers
finally fostering butterfly wings in
clear green in fine-sawn fringes
that flutter and fall at my withdrawal
mottled and golden

I am the living water
born in earth's dark recesses
stealthy as night I rise on the light
my shining is purer than light
I am reflective irresistible healing as
swift black night as sleep
euphrone
in all fluid forms I come rain
the giver of grain galaxy
milk of the black she-goat
the looser of care the red wine

dithyramb

I am the tree of life
men forgot Dionysus the twice-born
cut the tree let the sweet sap dry
wasted my wine
though I trod the press till my garments
were red as blood I touched the cold stone jars
and from their dark flowed honey-hearted wine
then they began to follow me again
over the broad-wayed earth

I took on my shoulder the cut tree
the dry stake of their making
they followed as of old to the mountain
now for the life of men on earth
they raise me openly above all the upturned faces
I hang on the dead tree
they take my life the fluid forms
water and blood flow down
now the leaves wave again
birds lodge in the branches

Calvary

when Christ went up to Calvary
his cross borne on ahead
a little wren went with him there
and sang him on his way

when he was nailed upon the cross
against the holy wood
the little bird his nest has built
for love of that high hill

(a vision seen as I woke this morning with part of the
poem heard, part lost, the last line clear)

MARY

what is this darkness
the shadow of the cross
stake driven in the ground of being
a sword shall pierce through thy soul also
do I stand here in darkness
not the kind dark of night
falling for the weary
what is this dark of noon
the light of midnight
when thy son was born
I stand in darkness
that no time can end
the whole world rocks
my child
behold thy son
heaven and earth shall pass away
I stand in this shade
that is the end of Man
why hast thou forsaken me

now I am no more woman
weeping and worn and old
I am a copse in spring
my bones lithe hazel wands
my breasts the tenderest buds
straining with leaves not green
but folded in fire and dew
sweet to the showers
the quickening drops the flowers
O my heart is young
with all earth's youth
on the spring air
leaf-nerved my fingers lie
pointed and poignant with life

wildness of all life
rest close as feathers
on my warm child's breasts
two hands to hold life soon
soon with smooth palms
to be a rest for death
child and wild wind flower
this copse of spring
is all my fire

what does this mean
the shadow is no more
sun conqueror shines among
the fires of dew and leaves
how do I stand
now I know this light
the dark received not
under the two-armed bough
that now
bears dead man's sole and living hope
I stand below and know
The Tree of Life

       ATONEMENT

I am
                      fear not

   I AND THE FATHER ARE
       ONE

   because I go to the Father

       ALONE

      this alone is known
    in the break of creation
      my God my God
       why hast Thou
        I am
       forsaken

to know at once
in one Man all that man is
in the life of separate body
must be at once
death of that body
or the endless process of making
in time would be over for ever
as it was in the beginning is

         NOW

FOUR MEDITATIONS FOR EASTER

I

Good Friday

let all be made bare
this is the preparation for prayer
the lace-edged cloth folded away
candle-sticks banished – for yellow rays
daffodils grow on the graves –
the cross alone   the cold stone
all who kneel are old   old
heavy with two thousand years
when men first began to learn
that sin is theirs
and suffering alone prepares
makes bare the soul
for death and birth
this child of earth
offspring of starry heaven

now the cross stands bare
the tomb is bright with sun
men above ground walk as wraiths
over the shining graves
look in each other's faces
and pass on

II

the underworld

the tomb in the hollow rock
is bodiless darkness
the sun has gone down to Hades
to shine among the dead
to shine through the poplar-leaf shades
no shadows they throw but each spectre
lifts his hand to his powerless head

how can it be where Apollo never dares
they behold in inexorable night
once more the light of the sun
these youthful sons of the Greeks
who bequeathed us clear light of the mind
no day-robber or lyrist this one descends
with wounds wounds that are red

with the fire of sacred altars
when day begins and ends
O let earth wait the rising of the sun
we cannot see you go the light
the light itself is amorous of the Greeks
and falls to carry back to mortal men
a torch new blazing the eternal Word

III

'he that liveth and was dead'

Christ is the glory of God
the fulfilment of eternity
the Christian revelation is
that it is possible for man
to sustain vision and reality
life freed of the necessary limits –
darkness and mystery

darkness and mystery
the substance of sorrow
incline our hearts to suffering
to rending our soul dismemberment
to break and devour the god
to take vengeance on the life-agony
all life here is robbery

the glory of God is boundless
nothing is lost
the order and adornment
builded and unbuilt
created and uncreate
this morning
the singing of birds filled His mind

IV

'touch me not'

chorus in the spare pearl-gray
the calm of early-born day
breaking into the garden of graves
is unchanged   is that why
singing of dawn-chorus surely as Orpheus
brings the soul in caresses
flute-notes and shimmering strings
to primal unmemoried birth

to hear the cry of 'Mary'
echo back from the sepulchre
the tenantless tomb in the birdsong of morning
is to know the peace beyond desire
where no fear advances
although the body shrinks
the sad robe dances
in the wind from Oriens
when the name is spoken
and the singing of birds fills the silence
that falls between them

EASTER DAY

I

'and the morning and the evening

now is the child of the vine
received new in the kingdom –
the denial the preparation
the cup of sorrow
are left on the earth he trod
the winepress and the sanctuary of God

the fun of being Dionysus
to turn water to wine
the sun with blood-red robe
and crown of thorn-sharp rays
abundant bread mountains and stars
waves of the sea smooth spread

the companionship of men and women
little children the girl still on her bed
amid shouts of laughter
the sacred human drama
is over with the last part – Adonis
strong with spring warmth at heart

risen – the very taste of life
is sweet to the giver
take the honeycomb adrip with nectar
kindle a small fire on the shore
walk before dawn when all
alive and dead are one

II

were the first day'

already the fulfilment the glory of Easter
with nightfall is over
the watchman who beheld the dayspring
in the crystalline window eastwards
must begin his star-measured vigil over again

the longing heart the loud cry of the lover
one voice the desired answers
the desert is watered and the deserted
is covered with soft feathers
risen again the rebuked waves
cradle the fishermen's boat –
yet all returns yearning and thirst and disaster

is it that Christ risen is *Majestas*
while in Lent he was among men
now after exaltation
our hope of consolation
looks forward again to the incarnation

'I if I am lifted up . . .'

III

of Arimathea

we have a strange office my friend
we who stand at the end
and at the beginning of life
that has neither end nor beginning

you gathered with your two hands
those simple swaddling bands
I the fair linen cloths with which I bound
the dead and wounded man

these coverings woven all throughout
with threads that cross the cradle
of old wood new grave in rock the stone
I rolled to close the hollow tomb

we two Josephs are plain men
all this is strange my friend
let us for once clasp hands
before with my good staff I leave this land

IV

ash

the behaviour of non-elements
is the concern of those who linger
most consciously where soul and consciousness
neighbour
being without the guard of reason
defences of experience
a certain willing for non-satisfaction
become a venture of attention

for this the Orphean twilight
between dawn with birdsong
and when the chorus falls under Apollo
is attentive   the inevitable
unexchanged glance as non-being
runs a swift plectrum
across the tentative chords that are
being's nerves undone new-strung
before the dove coos

dead with Christ from the rudiments of the world

PART TWO

CRUCIFIXION

passion is intolerable disintegration
each galloping atom
checked with a tight rein
on the brink of destruction
annihilation not annulled
in the mystery of human person
but in crucifixion

THE MANTIS

on Christmas Eve I lit a light
one candle in a copper stick
once my father held
and carried on his way to bed
one night of dread

my candle in the window stood
my prayer for living and the dead
who have no need of food
the flame burned strong with stars and moon
before the light I prayed within

and through the supple night came soon
another one on prayer intent
and on the sill with modest wings
laid smooth as two green leaves
and lifted arms prayed close to me
and silently as I

'AH, MY DEAR, BE SATISFIED'

a thousand times a day
is the bitter cup given
I taste and turn away
the cup stays by –
my grail

nothing above beyond below
simply the cup of woe
and this for me alone
no other may it take –
drink this

the hour comes and the full cup
all of it I drink
utmost dregs drain
is this the most love has me do
for you

O when my coward courage has drunk all
emptied the grail then passes out of view
a little space
is my most bitter soul
fulfilled

'EVEN THE LOUDLY ROARING LIONS'

the winds of heaven the great gales of God
crowd in the summer night rustle unceasing
mystic sheaves close inscribed tear-seared leaves
of lovers' letters that lend the stormy winds
a human music far above the trees
unmemoried surges for not one Dear Love
Heart of my Heart and O most Living Soul
but gives to tempests in their utmost wild
the stillness and the underlying rest
of those who learn to hold the brimming cup
unspilled to sanctify God in the heart

IN DARKNESS

when the light is withdrawn
not only the faithless
are left in darkness
but faith may remember
once there was hope
and singing of birds
in a withered winter garden
what is gone is immediacy
and intensity of being
the passion of poetry
the light that shone in the word

surety of faith in darkness
is this
that I can take in hand again
my sea-green pencil
and find a word among the sorrows
crowding because of oblivion
to write for my love who also
is acquainted with them
not cry for renewal
of those days of irradiancy
but declare the 'book of signs' is still open between us

EPIGRAMS

once long ago I bore a child
that did not see the sun
now I am old and the young child
is born anew in me

the child I bore and never saw
gone with life unbegun
shone in my sorrow as a star
that looks not on the sun

I know the silent cry
that greets my inmost grief
is for the child that learnt to die
before he drew a breath

THE WORD

I edge along the verge of the dug grave
that black oblong my boots go step by
step all the one day one night of my life
I walk by the open grave and do not
do not pass by for this digged pit is my
shadow to go by my side no creature
knows light without dark on one side the sun
goes on green earth on the verge of that dark
hole where deep dug earth groans within Peace
'I create the fruit of the lips' I am
that light unknown the clear shadow of God

CALVARY

this daily dying and crucifying
is the activity of living
will take no denying –
there is something artificial
about bringing all the suffering together
into one week called Holy
into one day Good Friday
three dark eclipsed hours
when God is dead

but it is a way of acknowledging
what is hid in the deeps of soul
discovering suffering to contemptuous light
exposing the stuff of contemplation
expressing gratitude for sacrifice
a way of revealing that sacrifice –
positive dying – is more possible
than negative living
which is dropping the cross
and not being lifted in agony

'AS HAVING NOTHING . . .'

suffering seeks to be fed
is always searching for sustenance
for something to sharpen insatiable longing
for the fulfilment of owning
there is no satisfaction

all is strange for sojourners and pilgrims
strange – and the best consolation
is recognition of poverty
when what seemed a precious collection
of intangible riches

the rewards and delicacies of thinking
communion with the solitary
the divine mind
(for we have the mind of Christ)
is tired and gone to dust

'SAND GRAINS AND GRASSES PROPHESY'

the instant crowned with fulfilment and death
is how I love now
unsurprised knowing a little beforehand
in quiet how it will be but not seeking to explore this
or questioning consciousness
which gives what is needful
from the hoard of all before and after
unconsciousness

how are we very alone
in givenness in imaginary choice
the relations within mind
and thought which make the individual
when the separate self is no more –
no need now of busy brain
the company of books in solitude
for one is never alone
never with others
this may be called
without desire

ONE WHITE FLOWER

the soul darkness to which mind
with patient labour and constructing
believed itself to be Lucifer
light-bringer creator
of luminous pattern
reason and gravity of intellect

with no trace of labour
the dark soil the soul
bore one white flower
a snowdrop maybe
that comes before spring
but is not by nature solitary

Lucifer enchanted gathered
his gold-grains seeds of reason
to shower the flower
explore its glory
the white petals enfolded their quietness
the desired withdrew into darkness

NENUPHAR

the void
the slant stalk
the flower alone
cupped petals colourless
parting for the centre
the sun

would you say lily –
lotus –
all that is sure is that suffering
alone opens the petals
imparts the vision
the radiance within
the heart of the flower

instantly with unfolding
suffering increases
no words any more
so poignant the rays
from the uttermost meeting
the inmost

AT THE NGARE NDARE

my only awareness of myself now is as a spectre
I live by the blood and being of forebears
as a seeing individual I cease
and am nothing but the vision
have only the nature
of those who see me

I am too sorrowful any more
to have the companionship of sorrow
and there is this reflection
in the eyes I look into
in the sleek flowing river at twilight
'like pewter poured out'

I remember another when the secretive
soft quacking black duck skims in
to the unrippled pool
and startles the water
one understands who took and held
kissed the backs of both my hands

'IT IS HARD FOR THEE . . .'

now my dear comrade in invisible arms
I who have kept close to you from youth
am outwardly old and all the harms
and thorns in the flesh we have shared
have lost point but the inmost pains
pierce to the heart of truth –
without your word for this sharpness
I could not stand

in this new dimension of age –
strange to me for I am young
to sorrow and heartbreak –
I want to speak to this quiet page
of my closest companion
in the hardship of living
the wrestling being

to tell it is well to be strong in suffering
the torrent of words of St. Paul
to run into all the caverns of mind
let that spirit struck by the power
of its own lightning lighten there
and find
the hidden things of God

ADRAD

a poem in the instant of conception
fusion of words with brain tremor is
endeavour of being throughout
as in the feats of ageing Odysseus
who excelled by the aid of Athene
the oar-loving dancers
the musical Phaeacians
for at that being-in-poem
all the laws of Jews and universe
cosmos and mortal creation
cease

they resume
after the touch of the Muses
with a fraction of difference
in the angle of one soul's response
to the empirical geometrical *Adrasteia*
adrad at the new song
as Jacob after his dream
the poet considers the best-loved stories
were always of Ulysses and Israel
until Christ stands before Pilate
and in his own body once and for all
breaks the law

ROAD TO EMMAUS

great rocks in the valley of shadows
receive on their surfaces reflected
light of your passing
although unrecognised you went by
grass green with the living water
of psalmist of prophets
Isaiah whose scroll you opened
read and refolded

trees dark mute with remembrance
attend the instant of revelation
at the end of the valley
when the breath of infinite gold
brushes their branches
and your form between the two listeners
is the shadow of God

(Poem for G.M.P. after long looking at her
painting on the night of her birthday)

REDEMPTION

the act of redemption
is unbroken
this Lenten labour to remember
brings in memory
the beginning of unreality
of piecing together of fragments
when mind and body are broken

soul atones
simply ceaselessly in silence
no space for fragments
no time for repentance
revelation in the human face
is the nature of soul
after music in society of fire

does religion begin with the cry of the lover
I want your body

ATONEMENT

'I believe'
four men give their thoughts
after this I ask my thinking heart
for a response to the numinous
the best for me definition
or limitation of the infinite
here begins the contradiction

I believe because the Christian faith
is
the mystery of being
manifest in the life of Man
my earliest revelation is the Word
according to the Gospel of John
declared to the child by the old
this Word is the reality of the symbol

my freedom   since I have fallen
into the power of the living God
to explore the unsearchable riches of Christ
in the given light of His knowledge and love
in the company of so great a cloud of witnesses
and – for he went to the mountain apart to pray –
in the poetry of aloneness

'BEHOLD, THE HEAVEN . . .'

(Ecclus. xvi.18–21)

the tempest shakes the invisible
the storm of the Lord
discovers the foundations of being
the ecstasy a shattering
of hedges and walls and fears
defences and commonplaces

if I did not believe
when you said
I saw you under the fig tree
the tumult of all we remember
the torrent resisted
would sweep me away

with the words come calm
faith in heaven opening
the light of your angel descending
into riven rocks and black
chasms of basalt
birth shining in death

CHRISTENING

'no lion can him fright'
night for him is no more
nor fine candlelight
the sacrifice is silence
roses stained with hues of life
one the pure white of faith
below the cross of wood

the child cried receiving the name
of the one who died
whose spirit a most conscious presence
visited us afflicted with longing
for the bearer of this name

for a space the Word is unheard
we may believe the burden of sin is shed
borne by another gone as a falling star
the cross is sorrow
even in the mingling of spirits
in the christening
in the altar fires and roses
the wise men's star

EASTER

this
is this the white glory of Easter
this refined purity of ash-white
land-
scape delicately decorated
with silver close-set thorns
waiting to wound
in frozen stillness
thorns here to crown all heads
living and dead
here sitting and forgetting find
in this final white fire
no desire

EASTER SUNDAY

do we know in deed and in truth
Christ is risen?
this we know and this we see
in eyes that look love into the soul
this is the light of life
shining from soul to soul
in Him who holds
all souls in life . . .

THE QUICK AND THE DEAD

dead and buried
I remember now hear in my soul and feel
the satisfaction with which we children
repeated these words

there is a green hill far away
on that top floor of the tall old house
would begin the day
though to be sure it was far away helped

I have a notion that children
for whom religion begins in the nursery
never know what it is
to be without God in the world

too many generations of them
run up the deep-grained stairs
clatter down again to play
in the sun on the nearby graves

perhaps it was not far away
the cross could have stood
on that great green mound
we scrambled to the top of
I'm king of the castle we would say in our play
can you think nothing   there I've thought it   we would say

VILLAGE CHURCH

I

men built ships in England ever to stay
in quiet anchorage of green fields
to withstand storms of sky of winter weather
unmoved ships of gray stone
with pillars of centuries old
gold sun bound underground
quarried carved to carry
roof wood
vessels to hold holy rood
God's Word to take in hold
all souls
mark of Emmanuel
God with us God with man
that man
labouring avails to build
temples of God

II

ark of the Lord stronghold
God's glory man's measure
many pass by who come to pray
make no stay
one heart through ages of long nights
changing lights of lost days
keeps steadfast faith
knight unknown bones
dust in Palestine stone-made
span-long sword shield lion at armed feet
for ever stowed in narrow niche
clasps on cold breast
casketed heart

he knows not days years prayers
readings of holy writ
sermon or psalm
only when two stand
with hearts at one beat
in praise before him
silence of pierced hearts
his heart of stone owns

BURNING BUSH

from the gravestones is played back on the soul
the passion of seven centuries of those who
also seeing or not seeing have looked on the tombs
from under this prescient arch –
here stand and take your fill of immortal
elemental cold – cypresses and sleek laurels
obliterate the day five-fingered ivy leaves
feel over a slanting monumental altar
the darling chubby-cheeked cherubs are sunken
obliquely glistening hail screens the air
scampers along the path instead of rice
they threw years ago for confetti
when the white brides were tearful

step out now from the porch to meet
breath-taking sting of ice grains
in one red sheet the flames
rush up the darkness of the mourning tree
the graveyard also has its burning bush

'THERE LITHE A KNIGHT . . .'

this is the place of gathering of all souls
who come as the gray thread of smoke that blows
when out the candle goes
and bends and twines and fades into the air

this red-gold ballad bed where the knight lies
and his wounds bleed as living water springs
and for there is repose
no otherwhere the girl with bowed head kneels

for ever by the wounded knight's bedside
and weeps for all the souls
now to this place of gathering O I come
before my flame's gone out because of love

for love allows me swift to follow through
that orchard where the falcon bore away
my warm and breathing soul
to that bedside and Corpus Christi stone

THE TRINITY OF RUBLEV

'I appoint unto you a kingdom'

on them falls not the light
as earth turns towards day
the light that falls as weight
on our opaque clay

on them does not fall
the dark that hides all
the mate of untold pain
the hold of dayworn brain

the kingdom appointed for them
is not of the light
or the dark of our sight
toil begins not nor rest ends for them

for those three who bend
with dwelling and aureoled head
with suffering hands that bless
with celestial and luminous dress

although they have entrance here
their presence and being is there
by grace of this cup they show
the kingdom appointed we know

THE CHOIR

Romsey Abbey from the Triforium

how are the stones transfigured
raised from inert being
grown lively stones
living on light
in the high-arched temple

do they transformed
into the splendid revelation
of arch sensitively erected on arch
clerestory transpierced by sky
the light symbolic of heaven

do they yet bear traces of sweat
the tears after eight hundred years
of hewers and masons
all who have wandered under
crown upon crown of round arches

with offerings of tears and fears
prayers for the dead prayers for the living
is not all this part of the transfiguration
this plait of fine-spun hairs
the abbess braided for her early grave

the skin of the face shines wan with tears
the garden waits at the foot of the mountain

A MEDITATION ON ANGELS

begin with Michael king of all angels
who stands at the head as Christ
in shining winged might

the sparkling stars are angels as are
white fires of waters cool
in the burning sun's noon

as the three holy children
with their whistling wind in the furnace
the breath of God's son

diagonal bands in the clouds are angels' dresses
the rejoicing outgoing of evening and morning
are the flames of angels' tresses

Gabriel archangel and holy
spirit of poets joins earth and heaven
with his two storm-plumed pinions

one sea-gull silver the other
dark as the fear of hearts lost
cast out of the host of angels

'AND NEVER AND NEVER TO DIE'

then there is the philosopher's angel
who guards the mystery of active intellect
his head is white with the shining
of reason the fusion of thought
with being divine mind
radiant in clay the faithless prey
of mortal torment

angel of silvery crown
and nerve-edged hands
that lift a little let fall
the veil lean now allow
on this eve of all angels
grace for the pain of the soul
sleep and my swallow-winged one

PHOENIX

'life brilliant and perfect'
hear this and believe
known by soul clear as light
as spring water the one note
of bird-throat in canopied night

quick the word pierces clear to the soul
wait now and listen
the soul unseen is near
clear as the vision here

of the silent bird that called
the lovenote into singing
in sunshine no more
but the soul in light shines clear
vision to soul in waiting

see my dearest the bird
vivid and virid-winged
crimson with quick-shed bright blood
the living heart of the rose

brilliant and perfect this bird

LOGOS

'The underlying unity in things' Heraclitus

this flick of the eye
fingertip touch
beyond relativity
must be caught
in swift retreat
or all is lost

what is left
is aloof notice
that everything is
inter-related
therefore dependent
henceforth   *désormais*

'with gravity dwindling'
emotions will be lighter
the high moon tides of nature –
antennae attentions
for the solitary spirit
directed

to the imperceptible
alterations
within the inescapable
principle even for poetry
relation
by unity within intuition

*'the unapparent connect is the real but underlying
unity of opposites and so of all things'* Heraclitus

THE CHARIOT

now I have come to the rim of the world
the pair of horses race round the curve
I crouch behind straining the long reins
my whip an arc in space

both white horse and black
beat the aether with forehoofs
sharp as arrowheads the hind
knock the old earth-rhythm
my soul does not look back
yet O black horse

the ground is scarce frost-cold
and fallen leaves are russet to the moon

O my wild horses is there no way back
see the four-spoked wheel
runs round on the darkening curve

ἐαυτῷ δὲ λαλείτω καὶ τῷ Θεῷ

(I Cor. xiv.28)

God by continuously breaking a link
in the established order of events
for the Vision and Conversion
(which necessarily blinded Paul)
proposes that God alive in man
will illumine by human hands

in darkness look to the other
the terror at the difference
the breaks in the links make
is not that the catena is undone
because so soon it is again the same
but because all things new suffer

because all things new suffer as before
the undifferentiated suffering is energy
to re-create the catena by heartbreak
in art quartet four-line Greek epigram
epistle unmake tradition yet
without gold links worn thin till

a thought snaps one and another
how know the new
there must be the expected
to protect the strange
these unlinked incompatibilities
mind brings in mercy to meet

Last poem.
25 January, The Feast of the Conversion of St.Paul, 1980.
Mary Casey died midnight 30–31 January 1980.

THE MIND OF CHRIST

not stretched on the cross
lifted up hung above the shuddering earth
free from the beginning
Logos of Godhead
the mind of Christ

Geometrical Relationships

AFRICA

THE BEALE

now my African home
that house of wood and stone
stands empty hollow alone

no candles shine
through long windows
to plain and forest

no lanterns lit
these nights in the attic
below the arid cold and snow
of our companion mountain
under Antarctic stars

SPRINGS COTTAGE

looks like a hayrick
wispy porches
windows with crosses
doors all open

sun and wind run in
touch red-cedar posts
roof-trees and rafters
waterproof grasses
neatly tied with string

by day white walls
cut on blue hills
by night roof-grasses
touching the stars

within are cups
pictures and stools
fruit in heaps in bowls
books in hillocks
books in rows

without
tiny twisted trees
crowned with thorns
among boulders and rocks
doves gravely walk
graven on golden grass

on the beam in the porch
on its black leather thong
the cowbell waits
for the wind from the hill

THESIGER
AT SPRINGS COTTAGE

one of the world's wanderers
stood at the door
no one within

grown old in solitariness
he waits to see
there are those

who take another path
another solitariness
remoter still

in time they come
break bread together
share a little wine . . .

Note: Wilfred Thesiger, the Arabian explorer

FIG TREE

why do we not fall as the leaves
at our life's end
when delicate veins restore
the ichor no more
to the core of mortal being
as the race of leaves
so the races of man are
then sweet and alight
all that is left of our living
falls earthward as leaf or star

but there is the body of love
this furnace cannot grow cold
turn to the umber and gold
of the tribes of leaves that are old
this solid geometry must lay bare
layer by devouring layer
all that has suffered the passion
of love in death the feathers of fire
quivering over inward arms
the limbs that dissolved and the soul

that left long ago forgetful of blood and bone
returns again to kiss
the honey-sweet house of the flesh
that is less
than the memories of dry leaves

SALLY'S DREAM

with dark I come back to Africa
where with high sun men of night walk
and keep for defence from heat's rage
the garment of night
only the dust with snuff stains
feet and hands' palms
my own dust of child's play
the long barefoot day

with each eve I come back
feel with fingers and fine-grained hands
the hills' mould in parched skies
between charred trees I go down
to watersprings and rivers
glistening over pebbles as fishnets
with pools and lava rocks dark
as men who invite night with fires

then for my content I take stones
lie down on the wide lion's hide plain
with all shining and far-shooting
stars for angels ascending descending
in my African night I remember
'I am with thee and will keep thee
and bring thee again to this land'

THE BROKEN FLUTE

after Theocritus' 'Flute of Daphnis'

I am not the pipe of Daphnis
a young girl it was whose soft
lips first pressed my mouth-
piece and woke the sound of music
hid in my hollow wood who
cast me on long voiceless voyaging
whereby my heart was broken
I had no clear note to answer
when I reached to her felt again
her fingers slip along my vocal reed
then she would make no offering for me
in memory of our close compact
nor even nail me to the wall
as her tribute to the Muses
so that when wayfarers looked on me
they would taste the joy of our first love-song

EPIGRAM

even a broken flute bound together with love
may give notes sweet as those from the throat
of an unseen bird in the troubled wood

FOR MARIAN

that morning of our moonlit walking
after the tawny the dappled leopard –
calling alone the long night –
over ground bright and yellow
and sable as the pelt of the hunter
we stepped softly and calling
and calling the leopard followed

we came by the river
singer of clear-flowing phrases
the living river the path
flaked with crescents and discs
of fallen moons and leaves
where between ebony pillars
water whiter than moonbeams

than filigree silver cirrose spun
clouds in azure springs severed
by iron-toothed scoriac rock
jets in jabots
bridal lace the shimmering shroud
from the tireless dance of the
bobbins

CONIES

in the branches of the trees
the forest's high solemnities
of dark and midnight Hyades
creak and scream the hyraxes
not human joys and miseries
vibrate in their discordancies

in the glooming moonless nights
in the full moon lost white nights
not round dense-pelted four-foot things
but all the wizened majesties
all the fire-scarred forest sings
with madness of tree hyraxes

and the longing yet unstilled
infinitely unfulfilled –
closer to eternity
than the kindnesses of day
pretty sunny solaces –
keeps concert with the hyraxes

A PAIR OF BUSHBUCK

listen my heart's love
there is no reason for poetry
unless you know too
the vision given
reflected in souls
in two clear pools
with ever so little division

stand with me here
the sun is not risen
tall grasses fed
with the tearless gift of dew
leaves shake overhead
the little curious ones run
among the yellow branches

a black face looking down
now from a thicket of thorns
a red-shouldered antelope comes
with ears wide spread
into our waiting pools
you see the high tread
lest he shed the sheen of the dew

he is pleased to stand in the glade
and delicate unafraid his companion comes
and we learn all their markings
where black and white stipple the red
flick of tail and turn of head
gruff bark and leap chatter of angry
monkeys and the dew undisturbed on the grasses

THE LEVERET ON LIZARD HILL

softest of all things new-born
gray hare lay still on gray granite hill
alone by the sun-warmed stone
unseen while buzzards scream
wheel white in bare blue

to live amid danger you must keep quite still
softest living gray grown in gray rock
unseen but hard round hoof struck
the soft form spurned aside
gives up life with small screams

FRIEND HARE

for William Cowper

whistling thorn eternal wailing
for there is no end to rending
Dionysus in us reddening
earth and soft fur
heartless sky over all

couched in grass warm
in her nest in the thorn
the hare rests dogs find
chase over stones
kill white teeth sweet

with hare's blood sad
in this clear moon-
bright night I stand
wait if I may on prayer
onto the lawn comes a hare

entranced I watch
this soft form warm
alert with quick turn
of head forepaws spoon-ears
raised then sweet on the grass feeds this hare

NOW I AM QUIET

now I must learn to be quiet
compact of passion
weak as a snared gazelle
the anchor cable is broken
but the wire noose holds my throat
I cannot pull grass
if I stand over the waterhole
I can take no water
the snare sees to that
young with strong limbs
wind racer
tawny coat stroked by the grasses
I go stiffly over the old plains
I go in fear of all –
I seek a place to die

THE UNVISITED NOOSE

I don't want to write
but black went the white
sun's noon heat tight
the footsnare drawn
the young gazelle thrown –
now you see only a slim bone
long dry looped wire –
two cruel toothed stakes
driven deep hold the snare

when you see with your eyes
such things the Fate
that each hour day and night
strangles stabs crushes
the golden leaping doe
the sharp-horned buck
you suffer with each of them –
the trapped terror first
twisting and flinging

hunger and weakness and thirst

SCHELTOPUSIK

senses sing to the music of absence
they have in the maker their own delicacy –
the soul's approaches are echoes
which crave the leisure of the philosopher –
to him always present
to respond to the small shocks
immediacy delivers most easily
in vision – hearing is more pre-selective
sound happens before it is heeded –
mind has innate scales
more than the audible number –
within startled yet not unprepared
perceptions – recognition of symbols
that are active but in abeyance
among the counterpoint of echoes

this scheme of recovery retention recollection
reculer pour mieux sauter
is the person not the persona
the chameleon changing paling and blushing
before inexorable unacceptable facts
the lizard that explores the inward approaches
and is never discovered

(Scheltopusik: *ophiosaurus* or glass-snake
'which has a peculiar distribution')

CHRYSOCOCCYX

when you see for the first time in a green tree
in a fine-meshed leaf-net in blue sky
a bird green as new grass in cold dew
and white as samite is or silver –
white as a fish's flank they fly
flickering over the wine-dark sea –
then you know a new being you –
bird for with green wings white tail you
fly in the bird's nerves in high tree
the bird's in your dark eye

MOUNTAIN WAGTAIL

the music and motion of water
is perfect
cascading holden
black by root-wall and rock
black from the source
on days undiamonded
by sun rays
there is a sinister Stygian shade
a suggestion in the dark of deep
subterraneous soul currents
unknown to the dry mind
but when the bird
made perfect of waterplay
adance aflash with the motion
of water so exact you say
dip and flick of tail is a
ripple of the beck in its stone bed
feet run run on the brink
you know if a wagtail runs so
on the margins of Styx
on the scoriac bank of the black
undertow of the soul
there would be no fear for you there

GREEN-BACKED HERON

for myself alone for none other no one
water receives reeds and leaves
greenness and plume upon well-head gloom
receives the sky's face the infinite space
with water's grace and duplicate dress
above and below the rushes grow
the palms are on high and hidden within
the subaqueous gleam at the pool's grassy rim
I place my feet neither wet nor dry
between the mirror and plentiful furrow

to the palm embrasure in reticent shadow
I warily dip my wraith-gray wing
and leave as I skim a double trace
of the saffron stalks on which I walk
in my marginal haunt by the liquid brim
for I shun the eye that must never rest
where I stand to seek my needful meat
on my cobweb mantle and reed-green pate
by the pendant screen of my adytum door
I musingly pause and am seen no more

SPEKE'S WEAVER'S CHANTRY

tenderest song heard
sweet sweet sweet bird
sing to leaf and twig cling
to sky-cut-in space
where lost chantry was
cradle inverted in-
tricate myriad loveknots in grass

yellow bird whispers
twitterer caresses
blue nick in leaf niche
here here will I fill
the void with a creel
sweet new green grass
flower-stalk after stalk
cut and bring with my bill

with stick and with stone
my shrine was broke down
but here in the gap
where leaf mourns on leaf
I promise to weave
a vernal contrap-
tion etherial complex
to contain upside down
a perfect world egg

I sing and I sing
with trembling wing
to tremulous leaves
that fear to be still
with my yellow feathery
breast to the sky
I promise promise promise to tie
with the kisses and skill
that are hid in my bill
a cock-cote twisted with sweetest grass

O only my beak has
art and love to entwine
a domed and waterproof shrine
where bird with shimmering wing
can chitter and sing and adore
aswing on bramble-sharp claw
and chirrup and kiss and confess
and adore more than ever before
a multiple true lover's knotted
incessantly twitter-wrought offertory nest

L'APRÈS-MIDI

extremity of dryness subtilises
density of moisture withdrawn
light rises higher
in the intensity of heaven's
empty empyrean

in scarcity of leaves shadows
are huge in the groves
not dapplings but glades
of white light
rocks unsolid shades

diminishing water
a more brilliant mirror
for the mystery of reflection
for exquisite enamelling
of green leaf and gold

laid on the floor of amber
smooth bed of umber
mud and moving palm fronds build
an emerald honeycomb
with no sweetness dry as mind

TURTUR CHALKOSPHILOS

'I consider'd a monotonous cadence' W. Blake

one by one
upon morning air
emerald drops fall
dove's measured prayer

now round and clear
hesitate here
falter return
run down sad scale

mourn into silence
take up again
green monotony
dove's intercession

in liquid gleam
notes descend again
broken chain
the prayer for rain

NARINA'S TROGON

for Valentine

in the branch-arched shade
where the gold suns fade
in the emerald caves
in the fanes of leaves
moons of malachite
ichor in airy
veins virid and fil-
igreed vivid and
crimson freaked
leaf-green narina
sapphire shimmering
living in leaf-roofed
rhythms of trees

touch of finger-twig
start of heart and thin
tissue skin gives wing
to a scarlet plume
a feather of sea-
green wing of the bird
so frail is the air-
y weft of the
rose-breasted passion-
ate hawk the leaf-green
narina of shade
of gold-fired suns
and high-arced desire

OPEN SKY

darling did you hear me say
all our birds are birds of prey
you and I together pray
morn and noon and night each day

with every prayer we fly
high from earth to sky
steely quills we prove on high
scan the world with hoodless eye

all our studies heretofore
are dust our crooked claws score
now that hunting is no more
birds no traces leave that soar

TRISTRAM

you see leaves fall
in the heraldic forest
pave the floor
with flakes of or
vert palm fronds slant
across the argentine
and fern-fenced rivulet
and all the orgulous
blue is hatched with sable
birds with wings of gules
blaze on the mazy air
and prank the boughs
with emerald-crested heads

but here there is no fall
no chaste and linear winter
never at all
to this armorial forest
comes the spring

ACACIA THORN

yellow tree
fallen on river bank
mats and strands of root
plucked from un-
bound hot ground
your fine-frayed watergreen
crests caress ash-dead grass

black man white ax
how you hew sun-bright boughs
chips of clean wood fly
sweet with tree's life sap
here lies lopped trunk
fresh brushwood near
unmoved the wind-rocked limbs

in my heart tree
where wild birds sing
shudders lets fall
mourning crowns of grieved leaves
on earth's tree fallen
O take life of this wood
thought stilled by the yellow tree

THE WHISTLING THORN

Birthday *Lied* for Goethe

hearken ear to the tree very alone
the wings' trill whirr of small bird above
wind's threnode on bleak spines
harsh the bark torso
cry death cry life press closer
the hearing ear the aloneness listens
the fibre of thorns has a new thrill

this day one comes to light
brings more light
crying naked
ich liebe dich – ich liebe dich

a ballad beginning to singing
singing on to naked deathday
lying *à outrance* the white body
the last unsung ballad

ROUNDING MUSUNGUKA

ride in among the granite hills
respite from drought
one day a rainstorm drew through
this tangle of rocks and thorns
find yellow ground pricked with green
flowers smaller than a mustard seed
these specks of speedwell blue

the eland of shining coats
gold with black leg-bands
on steep ridges stand entranced
in the new warmth of morning sun
giraffe turn down narrow heads
from their blue heaven
from afar Musunguka

has the mould of girl's breast
so fierce with flints it will never lose
the firm upward curve
behind in a hill harbour
a steading for Anchises
goats hang among the giants' skulls
unchanged his cattle stray without their keeper

COSMIC GNOSIS

when the passion of silence
is a white blaze
that outglares the fierce
horizontal equatorial Orion
is tenderer than those cloudy
galaxies so mildly milkily
gleaming beyond the bounds
of the million-starred Path
of Odin is a gnomon
pointing the zenith
the invisible sun's
finger signalling the zodiac

then this whiteness of passion's
recognition by itself
for itself alone
devours the mortal hours of sunshine
scatters their white ash
into eternal night

THIRST

peacock stream eyed with round stones
widening with night
all light is left in your dark
the delicate dusky sky
has lifted a trace of your blue
to you must all flesh come
to leave on your brink
the day of drouth

this is the drift where my loves come
the birds from arctic and arid wastelands
this night the black land on one hand
is crested with scarlet waves
from this I turn to the west
instantly down to the stream
and away an instant stay
on the infinite homeless sky

with chuckling cry
the sandgrouse come in
dip
fill each dry bill
with the peacock gleam of the stream
one cup of heaven
and return again again again again
to the constant sand

ABYSSINIAN LONG-CLAW

hopped fluttered at my feet helpless
in all this dearth of life
a little bird I stood to think
of the fatality of all that moves
on the old face of mother earth
hopped to a taller stalk and turned
my little one and sang
a cool clear pipe and showed
in the drab grass a saffron throat
an eye with brow distinct and bright

then all my care of coming day
of death for all that foot it here
was gone for on the desert air
with me was a quick song a liquid call

KENYA

they tell me it is frosty
I am poor
who live as do the gods
that are for evermore
where there is never hoar
frost nor hail where never blow
iced northern blasts and snow
dazzles far off as Thule
where rain forgets to fall
and dark Virgilian herdsmen
watch their sheep
on the harsh steep
of sun-bared hills

at night the piercing lights
of multitudinous stars
remember Jacob's dream
chance-laid a few stones seem
gathered for head by hands
and angel bands
climb or forsake the stars
on glacier stairs

SUNDAY AFTERNOON

surges with energy the grove –
whirl emerald spines of zigzag
electric-charged palms
hurl down from on high
tight-seeded dry figs thin
black fingers plash
splash in the pools crash on
crisp layer upon layer of leaves
strike and rebound from the branches

echoes with stir with rings
with showers of figs
with passion of poetry
swirl my mind my in-
visible veins full with fleet
sap of Bacchus
sun in quicksilver gleams
sparkles in diamonds on old
volcanic black stones

an angry clamour of birds one alone
my love with white breast tender my dove
with emerald-seeded wings

BOGO AND SPRINGY

I the white ox and full moon of the herd
dead with a weight of years now keep my head
that swayed through all my grazing life
still in this tree my horns stronger than trees
grow lichen as dead boughs I cannot see
with hollow holes for my full globed eyes
and yet this aged hanging skull is glad
when a cow proud as I now in her twentieth year
with udder shrunken that gave life to all
and horns a lyre growing on her brow
pulling the grass with toothless jaw comes near

FULFILLED

at the end of that long road
for this night
find the fabled fields
green peace green feast green rest
Dionysus god of kine of drovers
lithe and horned formed
when he pleases strong as a wild bull
he goes among them
this night
couching tired breasts
in nests of soft wove grasses
taking their midnight breathings
catching the stars above the cloven peaks
between the horns of the most aged cow
the herd would follow
on the inimical starched white plain
the god rests flank to flank with her
for this one night

THE LIFE-GIVING EARTH

eagles that nest among the stars
descend towards evening
when wind from the desert races
clean as a whistle up rocky precipices
runs up the heavenly stairs as a many-
voiced fountain of airs
for the play of the wide-winged birds

to balance on the invisible
is the heritage of the martial eagle
with tilt or half-turn of pinion
revolve on the zenith
ride down the falling gale
straight as a wall
meet a flaw and ascend in helices

earth of the heaven-born eagles is graveless
bare of death as a star
no white bones among rocks no cairns of stones
no hunger in the high empyrean
for a warm hare cowering in the grasses
gazelle fawn flat on red earth
to escape sight inured to all suns

HOGMANAY EVE

'To the mistletoe the New Year'
from far and near and everywhere
the spirits of the dead who live
are dancing through the sunny air

a writer long ago has said
yet free of date as are the dead –
imagine light invisible
and you see spirit so my head

this New Year's eve is all alight
with those I love in conscious flight
unseen and near and everywhere
present and instant clear as sight

as Homer sang from friend to friend
so sing I now at this year's end
'dearest of all men to my heart'
whose hands compelled my head to bend

MODULATIONS

FOR K.P.

(after reading her diaries)

you are in prison
the bars are hateful age
same as the east wind
this makes man like a wheel
no more to regard heaven
the racing clouds
those tragic gray eyes
clamped to the ground old friend

'the same the same the same'
day by day is writ down
the last penitential years
yet through that criss-cross of bars
sun warms fire burns
comfort for shoulders and shins
day by day there is 'rest and reading'
'tea and evening'

never one day you left out the wind
the quarter and way of it
now you go free as the unrecorded winds
with seagull wings

T.F.P.

in the morning mists a gray figure
hid with stones amid the grave-fed grasses
headhigh tassel flowers etched on mist
holding sickle crooked scythe on shoulder
he stood a ghost arisen from those tombs
and grassy fog-draped burials and said –

'you don't know where to start
'twould be better if there was a path
an' 'tis so wet too' –
dejected scratched his head
we spoke a little while with graveyard pauses
until he ended cheerily turning from me –
'ah well not to worry'

deep in earth enjoying the sensation
of final obliteration
into clay resurrection
into tasselled grasses
the dead man said –
'I rest well as I am Jackie
The Book is well hid by these gentle
grasses'

Note: T.F.P.'s gravestone is in the form of an open Bible

OFFERINGS

for Ll.P.

here are pomegranates for you Llewelyn
sprung from the blood of the god Dionysus
out of Africa with a word and a stir
of kindred blood bright as you
stained your doorposts
long ago

all morning I copied poems
of Clare till all country England is here
these I bring with the polished fruit
for your sunshine to fall on
with Will's Montacute legend in Africa
and Lucy's in England

the living thee living remember
       Llewelyn

NO MORE

for Alyse dead, August 27–28

now I come again as of old to sit at your knees
but forgot is the folly of girlhood the roughness and storms
I only want to say do you remember –
I want you to take again as then you would
from me the pain and anguish
of being alive at all

our friendship made a concord between passion and reason
yet mind and heart often took other council
went along ways that could never meet or cross
but there was an answering wildness of blood
I shall never know again a kinship
in most dark melancholy
an utter blackness in our bright coursing blood
that mingling in intellectual cold
took away sorrow the unconsolable
grief of earth-life of
woman born to woe and unredeemed
froze the despairing emotions
wrought despair itself –
this bitter mingling –
into the beauty of Greek sculpture
reflective cool unmoving
conflict in full light

an uncommitted interplay
not daring to stay but convening
in a swift libation
of that sharp wine of the heart
finding some succour in our *amitié*
(and must I this betray)
in the brow of the down above
that high-up attic window
the red of the black-souled poppies
the cry of a gull

do you remember
or am I alone in this
for if you do not there is no meaning
in those last words you wrote –
forgive me and remember me

FOR MAY AT MONTACUTE

'as the leaves of a tall poplar tree
twirling the thread
their fingers move as they sit'
so now I think of the lacemaker
with fingers busy dark head devoted
to the intricacies of delicate threads
butterflies from her hovering hands
flowers and timid fawns live
in the grace of this civilised art
of sheer adornment and she
is free again in the garden
her feet to run
where all her skill began
with the twining clematis tendrils
morning and sunlight of primrose
keen quiver of leaves in air
the network designs on the lawn

KATEY GREY

as children and wise old women
we were together
while your dark Indian hair lived
its own life your eyes looked
once and again as Charles looked
mocking eternity

the sun is dying we are told
the ageing earth is growing old

SIBYLLINE

when I came here the leaves were not born
that now attend me on my bare floor
fall undestined in the ruffled air
gather and disperse on the grass

I want to ask them what their secret is
curled and observant at my feet
perhaps they whispered this to the summer winds

maybe wave-washed with unshed tears
I do not hear their answer
yet I am glad of their fickle company
as we keep together our sibylline silence

DRYAD

waiting to be cut down
the twigs shine with rain
from rows of clear spheres
drop one here one there tears
of the dryad
grace of the living wood

I sit at my table
write hold a book on my knees
know by my side the tree's
suppliant flower-tipped twigs –
you know the pliant down-bend
of boughs that lift at the end

tender as ferns these flowers
green for hope
between them the folded leaves
feel their first rain
the coming rustle of olive shade
will not be spread nor fade

BRAMLEYS

my hands are still full of apples
too full to hold
cool and round in twos they grow
my fingers enfold one   one falls
I reach   the best smile beyond reach

the red ladder leans steeply aslant
among the red apples
bright as a storybook picture
picking apples
I climb

losing time in the leaves
losing my separate self become
one in the small dangers scares
triumphs of the one generation
apple gatherers

WIZARD

that little thorntree printed on the sky
could never thrive
in the bitter drive
the grind of salt-grained wind

in empty mind
on nebulous heaven
the driven tree
must stand still as despair

and in this image of the winter
tree with my heart's eye I see
why thought with thorns
and shrinking all one way

be it November bare
and all the year
of leaf and life gone over
wrenched wind-whipped yet a tree

and I remember –
do you not now –
the song of hawthorn bough
and all the blossoms stars

favours and splintery rays
pulled down from heaven
to overarch your brow
my white thorn bough

WARRIOR

I

the door is open wide –
earthward bends the year –
think on those who died
that it may be so

on the floor the leaves
perform their noiseless dance
apples fall and roll
down the long parterre

wait beside the wall
grave green pyramids
tell me by the open door
I need have no fear

warrior who stands here
this most ancient tree
bears neither sword nor spear
with his shield saves me

II

after largesse of apples
little toasted leaves like cornflakes
gild the shrunken grass
edible unlike the oily unpalatable
pool below the pear tree

still single apples fall
still thick-leafed shield above me
September sun somnambulant
steeps my faded pleasure-ground
I and the tree of a hundred winters

together in fair trance – I do not sleep
or wake think or let my heart long
for the lost grace of song
in this warm rest I am not here
and I lie here for ever

STILL PAUSES

every road is the way to Hades
now my thrush who sang me
'new suns shine among the dead'
who sung those broken phrases
of our lost spring when I could sing
no note of my love's song
my thrush is dead
that came with every daybreak
with speckled breast for food
and viewed me fearless through
the window-pane her eye calm
and dark – she fed at leisure
as the thinker who attends the soul
has those still pauses

WANDERERS

from this dead tree return to another
beside the hand-ax track
where death and life pass
into singing grass

upon the tree one day or another
caught on unbending bone
hawk falcon far-ferried red kestrel
drawn to the ferreous wood

from edgeless space
in this fire-scoured plain
where mazy thorn brakes cower
there is no other foothold

this tree tempered by flame
blasted by sun is siliceous
black-patched with charcoal
a strained figure for purgatory

and sharp-winged falcons
from narrowing polar circles
to the full rondure the equator
in passage pause in their skimmings

alight on this dead tree
as the hawk on my almanac clasps
with cold claws the old bough
and his yellow eye re-minds me

WINDS OF SPRING

how clean are all the winds of spring
nothing they have to whirl away
no leaves to twirl in widowed waltz
no saraband upon the grass
no devil's dust and castaway
of the decamping year
there is no doubt the winds of spring
make the best sport when all is bare
no rags and tatters no wild tears
no rustling when the high trees surge
only the notes of feathered throats
whistles and pipes and flutes and chirrups
defy the gale signal the naked earth's new verge
life tumult winged upon the empty wind

WIND-HOVER

the hawk caught on the calendar
with the west wind would fly away
the frantic paper leaps as high
as spiral wire will allow

the window is fast latched now
the paper month falls meekly to
with spotted fox-red wings heart-spread
the kestrel grips his dead tree wood

does he not turn his yellow eye
as I do mine up to the sky
June ended he will quit this place
and I shall lose his still balance

JESSED

I sit here on my rosewood chair
touch with my fingers
feathery foxglove flank
on the last June day

look then to the sky the cloud-race
shadows scamper the land is alive today
through the transparent rectangular prison
a glassy shield I see

in footless flight the falcon
wing swerve quiver clean glide
promise fulfilled signal given
the bird on life slides down wind

the spirit healed and rent anew
by cause the course on high most lost
while libbard fox with stiff brush
pads under the barred gate

AN INSTANT SINGLE

so long since I've talked with you
all vistas open not one recession
along green alleys
through brain's byways
closed by a word-pattern
some form of smouldering Eros

you answer
the surge of fire
must be my poem
but this is not the full
consummation
soul within soul

the double flower
an instant single

HEDGEHOG

I wanted to say a farewell
to the long days of honied light
the crystalline white
nights of hot July
but instead it is the one
O well defended with his
cheval-de-frise of spines
killed by night
left for my morning eyes to meet
with the unexplored light
for him my elegy
dead in the road –
feeder in damp ditches
gipsies' provender
I look to see your lean black feet
again in Hades

THE VISIT

my love came in time of daffodils
and hunger of sun for earth loves
the dark of sacrifice slanted
against immutable gold
there is a wergild
all pay
who with body and mind
do disobey the law

for the pain in her torn side
tore up the flowers
showering gold in the gardens
broke our bright rays with dark shafts –

the grave of waiting
is not greater than the wrench of meeting
when you are cut out
and I ran from the locked glass box

THE FALLING STAR

now I declare myself to be
John Donne your heir
in this aire-angel race
of poets metaphysical
'that thou may'st know me
I will turn my face'
to you before I die
and in my heart I cry
you intercede for me
in love and death
whose mighty company
is all we own
together and alone

that thou may'st know me cousin
now I cry you
let fall on me your wild divinity
'whoever gives, takes liberty'

CALYX

the blessed gods the happy ones
had their cupbearers
youth and spring
girl-boy Ganymede
the puffing smith limping
placatory and maker
of fireproof merriment

when nectar grew too etherial
for mortal and ageing earth-dwellers
envious of the Olympians
ran from land to land over
high mountains and golden-
flowing rivers flowery
Dionysus looser of care

his own cupbearer the wanton
vine twining his fingers tendrils
and leaves aspiring with his shadowy hair
another also sitting at meat
is his own cupbearer
shares the red wine with his friends

FESTIVAL

bees priestesses of Apollo's oracle
at the foot of Parnassus
murmurous through the Communion
high over the harvest sheaves
the purple and gold and vermilion
of ripened flowers and faded
festoons of English Dionysus' ivy
weave between pillars yellow as honey
their sibylline sayings

bread of Demeter spread the fruit of the vine
on the white altar cloth
low to the wafer and flaming wine
the human priest bends
to transmute the earth-born food
into flesh and blood of God
of itself the silver cup slips in his hands
libation is poured to the gods that are for ever
the fair linen drinks a violet stain

the small winged priestesses with hidden stings
sing their assent to these holy mysteries

THE SAINT

now all leaves fallen
little nests exposed
spring-built in bushes
on sky-high branches
still strong but thrushes'
round cups cracked
dead leaves in these cradles

I must return in the season
of expiation no less bare
there than here all must suffer
alike the dryness
the cold at heart
I must go through the ruined choirs
solitary my love

because of you the birds sing now in Hades

THE TWINS

to rediscover in language
the simplicity of the heart's anguish
hot thought is endowed with reflection
hand leans on quietness

even the twins death parted
who never went one from the other
happy together in the hollow oak tree
in alternation

Zeus gave life to each
they shine above the earth
but not together the brothers
walk in the light of the sun

NECTARY

a word will not lay one flower petal on paper
the colour form process procession
earth-contact air water sun
the run of impressions into one word

the shape of the whole flower
balance fragrance silence
petals pecked by sparrows
we who weep are present with Herrick
something more than Wordsworth

the answer is before the question
song not name or word
'where the bee sucks
there suck I'

there are many shapes
even among petals
do you guess the print of the one I leave
here an outline on the paper

NO STONES

here I stoop down
and write upon the ground
of the strong Roman town
where all doors closed before
open not open wide
but are no more

we trod the pavements
love inlaid
and made the city walls
tall houses and church towers
fade into light
within the white

glory of our dismembered living
the independent principle of life
burning in being
is not ours to command
or to dispense and to know this
is to stand once before Him
uncondemned

MEDITATION
ON THE EVE OF CHRIST'S NATIVITY

among the stars also reading astronomy
I discover a literary serenity
in dusty darkness in-
finite distance discover in-
ward solitude absorbs all
I no longer need as you bade me
pretend to be pleased
that part is done for me
now the fiery passionate stars
are far within
that act is over
I can be naturally pleased

and the solitude
the gentle dusty dark with Canopus
the unattainable radiance
receives all pain agony of living in-
to unmeaning ages –
before the empty quarter of being
I make the gesture with my left hand
the renunciation of fear
that is of the task-master Duty

THE UNSEEN BIRD

lightly love winged my word
gaily I let the bird-
blood in my leaf-green veins
sing in the pen-pricked word

'shining' I writ the word
air on a sudden stirred
scared by the wings of love
shadow of feathers whirred

claws of the unseen bird
curly hair lightly stirred
pricked with the nails of love
head bent to shining word

CHINESE

under the window in the early morning
gravely writing Chinese characters
close by me on the ledge alighted two doves
their feathers bright and smooth
one living amber eye turned on me
scorned my indoor practices pen paper
pile of heavy much-handled books
with clap of wings they flew into blue
indifferent heaven left me low featherless
to bend again to the grief of Chang O

THE NATURE

this is the nature of love
that one word on the vibrant wire
through rain and wind
takes all the soul
as though the love of all
high poets and lovers of the world
all their forsaken lost cold love
spoke in her grieving words
I cannot bear it for the leaves

now I look at them
in their tossed weariness whirled and
helpless gale-driven and bound
and say – there is nothing but woe
or only something besides that lets you know
it was not always so

and this besides is to know
that one who is wild with pain
is tender to torn leaves gentler to them
than nature or God is
this is the nature of love

FLOWN

this is a wild bird darling
green feathers heaven's bestowing
do not stroke her back and wings
they will not suffer such things
not man's handlings
will the bird allow

but how can I know
how will she know I love her so
if I may not show
with touch of hands –
heart that forbids you grow
old and narrow with woe

no darling that is not so
my beat is as wild
as the wings of the bird
until we no longer behold
the light of the sun and feel
the tears of the claws of the bird
no more

UNBRAILABLE

my falcon is wild
waiting on death
astraining on her jesses
leaning thin to the wind
moping with trailing wing
claws cling to the world's rim
eye attains heaven

do not forget wild one
I kneel to and worship you
as none other has worshipped
a well-trained falcon
unless it may be once
the hieroglyphical Egyptians

WISP OF SNIPE

customary cultivated serenities scatter
the touch of Dionysus electrifies
wildness unloosed undoes rhythms
schooled by being's limits
cut round bodily toes fingers
expected forked outline
currents uncap brain cells
nerves stream as meteors
there is nothing but this experience

the instant not looked for
yet all before an exact preparation
hard road trod dormant trees suppliant
planets' gleam rose-fire west
hold off nightfall
– he snatched one crumb and was off –
hurrying waters low gurgles
up from the marsh one one more
here again one dark vibrant wing
very ground speech life's tongue click
from bird's beak to reach back aeons

FOR A BIRD
DYING ON A LOVE-LETTER

swallow at dawn would fly
out through her narrow door
to ply across goldwash sky
this day wing spread wing caught
the bird hung by her own
well-built safe home

I cut with a sharp knife
the nest-traps' mudrock wall
warmed the waning life
with my breast my palm
knew the bright eye knew death
in each small shaky breath

where could I find healing
for the torn bruised wing
leg bent back and claw
that no more could cling
could love do this thing
where her hand had been

leaving the name of love
of all birds' spring wooing
there I laid bluewing
still with unfallen head
with sky-cutting tail spread
with anguished weak breathing

O by my soul you keep
let the loved bird have life
when the sun rose and lay
warm on the shining wings
the bird took that dark way
by which no one returns

GREEK

the gods on earth
going about the business of being mortals
always recognise one the other
do not desire praise of another
nor need to be humble –
though they go lowly
as little earth scholars
or though they take glistening wings
and ring the mountain that nurturer
of keen eternal snows

the diamond in the dark earth-bent eye
splinters the instant
meeting the gentian
blue from gazing on heaven

win from Pindar
words to lighten on the stature
the fulness of manhood

the eagle even on Etna
is entranced by the golden lyre

PAEAN

when I would sing my paean
new song spring song
that for many days now
has been saying write me
there is only silence
echoing ἰήιε παιάν παιάν

if the very gods need a healer
to bind their wounds of love
can I teach my open ones to tell
spring is in the garden
well – let me be silent then
as the cherry tree

today the dry twigs are set
all along with groups of leaves
and small sealed buds
and the black-winged bird
waits among them
with no spring song

THE VESTURE OF FOG

μακρὰ χαῖρε

here where I lie
before another summer's open eye
confounds my sigh
with blossom's innocent snow
soundless let me go

this will not do
not if desire
be clear altar fire
lit in love may I uncumber so
the ardour of the self-conscous flame
has not fulfilled the art of undelight

each breath renews the claim
throws a dry dust out of all the past
incense on the wish to die
to be no more
those who are so
most livingly they throw

their ashy incense storax myrrh
on my sweet wish
to keep it fresh

KOUROS

the figure which stands at the beginning
of Greek human sculpture
before Apollo Kore
charioteer Athene
Zeus and the glorious horses
is most haunting
on the horizon where mind
meets that which knows not stands

the youth with archaic smile
one foot advanced with hands
with massively moulded shoulders
receiving the irradiance
the fires of gods who uncaring
yet caring a little
let fall on the shores of earth
some seeds divine

give him one glance
before hurrying on to Kore
to Hera and Hermes
you are undone
from him grew the beauty
perfection and fulness of sculpture
here – while his stiff-limbed figure
young archaic smile
break from the spring and origin of life
when all was fire

before memory froze immediacy or men
heart-worn
learnt longing for Lethe

EPIGRAMS FOR A YOUNG GIRL DEAD

I

Janey whose heart was so light
she could run over the mowing grass
and not offer the wind a pollen-grain
betrayed by jealous stones on the mountain path
that her quick tread did not press
fell six hundred feet down the precipice

II

Janey eldest of three sisters
in love and wit surpassing
on her way to the mountain top
slipped over a sheer drop
and left our hearts for the house of Hades

III

Artemis inimical to the chorus of nurses
as they ascend by her hunter's path
to the heights strikes with gentle dart
the dearest who at that touch descends
the way of no recall to Persephone's keeping

IV

'the way up and the way down is the same'
may it be so for Janey who on her upward course
suddenly found herself in the abyss

'BEHIND THE MILL'

'God loves the crafty ones . . .'

let go your reason and good sense
the air itself will be less dense
and bird will build a bough to sing on
in the lack of pride and reason

dawn is new before redemption
feel the essence in the thing
fifty years of lent betrayal
gives the heart a limpid spring

study fast and concentration
disarray the first born sun
every word is contradiction
as you prick it with the tongue

take for your vision blood and bone
the very air you ride upon
will build a mind for clear unreason
bird to sing and bough to rest on

FREE

not one of the unresolved opposites
not the mystery of the Trinity –
can interfere with the in-
dividual human will
so John says
and so no doubt many say
in our modern permissive way
till the uninterfered with will
is dull as litter left in gutters
at the gray pavement edge

weeping weeping the soul
calls down the dark of sleep

NO THREADS CUT

you could call it disentangling
no threads cut
merely drawn taut
by invisible tension
the pattern discovered limpid
as when ripples an instant
untrouble   timeless reflection

the single thought
in isolation not nature's
is not for the mind of the poet
who thinks with his senses
nerves contact of skin with air
water weight of light

a whole inwrought network
dappled as deer as woodland
with sun-discs multiplied
single only sudden
panic terror in crowds
lyric a snipe started
into flight from waterside

CHINESE POEMS

I

strive to enjoy spring's flowers
but forget not the time of our happiness
living I shall be sure to return
dead I will be sure to think forever of you

II

spring dawn

sleeping in spring one sleeps not in the dawn
when far and near the many birds are singing
but night falls with a rush of wind and rain
and showering petals of how many flowers?

after Meng Ho-Jan

III

night thought

brightly the moonbeams glance about my bed
to me in dreams a glittering hoarfrost shed
lifting my head I gaze upon the moon
my head sinks back and I remember home ·

                              after Li Po

IV

returning home

now the old man is drawing near his home
his hair is thin but all here is unchanged
the children run to meet him know him not
and laughing ask from where the stranger comes

                       after Ho Chih-Chang

V

night: mooring a boat by Maple Bridge

the young moon sets rooks caw in the frosty air
across the river fishermen's fires burn
after grieving sleep
now from beyond the city of Soochow
the midnight bell of the monastery knells
to the stranger's boat

                           after Chang Chi

JACK-GO-TO-BED-AT-NOON

'light simultaneousley present throughout the sphere'

'the relation of spiritual unity to material multiplicity'

take this for Corpus Christi
this gold-stayed gossamer globe
cobweb cups held up each one stiff on
gilded diagonal radii
whole perfect on strong green stalk
cut off from the root
deep in ground that raised
sunflower to sun rays
before sacred day wanes

this yellow goat's-beard
becomes one enthralled sphere
symmetric cups bright in air
pinned each to a hid seed
invisible at spanless point
spun-glass fistful finer than mind's
metal-work fashions
hold on high with one close-lipped cold breath
the cosmos is undone

THE UNDIVINED RESPONSE

poetry *is* the immediacy of philosophy
the unscientific dialectic of soul
within the silence of her own
nature and intensity
which are metaphysical
energy active reflection –
contemplation surprised
by something vivid unimagined
glances aslant the instant
heart bounds the impulse to tell
is unbound no one understands
no one ever understands
yet the poet must say
the vision not of brain
and analytical reason
but of life compact in clay
on the wide-wayed earth

the sheer and glaucous arc of crested wave
unbroken
the surge of horse and rider
the undivined response

FOR R.S. THOMAS

'after so many deaths I live and write'

frescade follows frequencies
in the dictionary
the title a trifle uncertain
with a hint of derivative
even where Kierkegaard is not absent
repetition

although we all draw from one another
our sequences are free as the skylark
prone to look before and after
so the caged panther on the prowl
does not precede the snow tiger
in *le jardin*

church porch points to the prudent pastor
we move to Herbert's falconry
hurt heartful and thankful
hear the blackbird's pensive antiphon
his song season all but over
with eyes lidded

how fresh O Lord how sweet and clean
are Thy returns . . .

AUDEN DEAD

'nor sorrow take his endless look'

when I tired
at my side
at my shoulder
the head of a poet came to me
wrinkled and heavy-grained
round the brow as elephant whale
Moby Dick the white Boran bull
told Auden dead
having left that island called Teos

something is gone from the earth

OVER THE RIVER

for Sylvia

all the year I waited for a token
now three days from the end
when every window square is birdless
blurred cracked if not totally broken
gray with aged ironies
that will not quicken

when I disobey the Zen
that declares there is no mirror
and polish the heartless glass
my dormant attention is woken
by the passing between two
as of fish and frog footmen

winter cold hands something spoken
before the form was changed
to remind me before the year dies
everything which was there before
is there now in love seagull rook dove
O across the quilt of plover one swallow

NEBELGLANZ

the interplay of same and different
is the tension of living
comparison then is essential
desire for surprise
springs from the recognisable
the imaginary constant background
in incomplete recognition

day involved in fog at the beginning
absolves from the nakedness of light
one tree steps forward a pace
an angle of roof cuts the void
there is protected isolation
breath kept body quiescent
no necessity for interaction

small birds are dumpy
nothing is surprised

GEOMETRICAL RELATIONSHIPS

you will not let me be
because of your silence and pattern
never to be again so
low in the early light you rest
so still only moving on the spines of the urchin
sun caught on green thorns
a clean triangle of white
on sea-rolled lilac stone
the mandala from Maine
out of the cold Atlantic
in the Chesil pebble's shadow
and sleek red marble

these for central symmetry
their jagged barriers
on my window-ledge are apart
from the fellowship of ocean stone and spine
they are dry primordial land-wrought
man-carved hand-ax
shaped by what crouched progenitor
gone to dust
this chipped dead African stone
eating no light and last green quartz
that diamonded angular I gathered hot
from the desert for love of the sea

PAIN

'ready to be anything in the ecstasy of being ever'

this regular nocturnal ruler pain
keeps a most silent council in the brain

I return to grief and pain
the cosmic rays are buckled in the brain
the star whereon my soul is charioted
has suffered shipwreck in infinity

the dawn begins the robin sings
there is being in the little things
the fabric of another day

FOG

'in this unknowing knowing
well content to be nothing . . .'

fog dissolves the texture of light
rays and radiance are alchemically disseminated
direction has no existence
far and near are not

yellow flowers grow out of space
in a Chinese painting
with added angles and proportions
because of no shadows

knots of leaf buds are in pointed tension
this is their instant of ecstasy
pressure in yin and yang exact
grass is surfeited with jade dew

on the way back to where there is nothing
I am well content in the vesture of fog